Coping
with
Your Partner's
Jealousy

Nina Brown, Ed.D., LPC, NCC

New Harbinger Publications, Inc.

Distributed in Canada by Raincoast Books

Copyright © 2004 by Nina Brown
               New Harbinger Publications, Inc.
               5674 Shattuck Avenue
               Oakland, CA 94609

Cover image © Corbis
Cover design by Amy Shoup
Edited by Karen O'Donnell Stein
Text design by Tracy Marie Carlson

ISBN 1-57224-368-6 Paperback

All Rights Reserved

Printed in the United States of America

New Harbinger Publications' Web site address: www.newharbinger.com

06   05   04

10   9   8   7   6   5   4   3   2   1

First printing

This book is dedicated to my family.

Contents

Chapter 1
Your Jealous Partner and You   1

Chapter 2
Triggers of Jealousy (Immediate Factors) and Why They   17
Don't Matter

Chapter 3
Why Your Partner Turns Green: Some Self Factors   37

Chapter 4
Past Experiences   57

Chapter 5
Family of Origin Experiences   73

Chapter 6
The Jealous Partner: Clingy and Reactive Styles   89

Chapter 7
The Jealous Partner: Manipulative and Exhibitionistic   111
Styles

Chapter 8
Suggested Coping Strategies   135

References   157

Chapter 1

Your Jealous Partner and You

Note to the Reader

The information in this book is presented to help guide you in understanding yourself and your partner. Nothing contained herein is intended to support physical or emotional abuse. If you think you may be in an abusive relationship, I strongly encourage you to seek help and guidance from agencies and professionals in your community who are trained in how to help victims of abusive relationships.

I believe that it is important to use gender-free language, and so I have chosen to use male and female pronouns in alternating chapters. Hence, in chapters 1, 3, 5, and 7 I use male pronouns, and in chapters 2, 4, 6, and 8 I use female pronouns. In every instance, both genders are included.

—Nina W. Brown

Sara had had a wonderful time at the party. It had been such a good evening that Sara did not want it to end so soon, so as her boyfriend, Todd, drove her home, she asked him if he wanted to stay awhile after they got to her apartment. She was surprised and shocked when Todd said no in a very curt and abrupt way. Sara immediately asked what was wrong, but Todd just glared at her and kept driving. Sara kept trying to find out what had produced Todd's mood, which was so different from the one he had displayed at the party, but he would say nothing. When they arrived at her apartment building, Sara once more asked him to come in, but he just told her to get out and shut the car door. By this time Sara was in tears and feeling very upset. Todd just drove off, leaving her standing on the sidewalk. Her evening was now ruined, and all her good feelings about the party were gone. She could not imagine what had gotten into Todd.

Over the next two weeks, Sara kept trying to get Todd to talk to her about their relationship and discover what his anger had been all about, but he kept evading her. Finally, after several attempts to talk with Todd, and many tears, she called his best friend to see if he had any clues or suggestions.

Todd's friend, Bill, told her that Todd was convinced that Sara did not really care for him, and that he was trying to keep from being hurt any more than he was already. Sara was perplexed, and she asked what had given Todd that notion. Bill told her that Todd had been upset ever since the party, where he saw Sara showing interest in another man. Sara didn't know what he meant, and asked for more information. Bill told her to talk with Todd and hung up.

Sara didn't know what to do, but since she really cared for Todd and thought that he cared for her, she decided to try once again to talk with him. She called him and, when he picked up the phone, she rushed to tell him that she had talked with Bill. She said that she wanted Todd to know that she really cared for him and wanted to work out whatever was getting in the way of the relationship. He agreed to meet for coffee the next day.

At their meeting, Todd was initially remote and detached. When Sara told him what Bill had said, he tensed but did not become angry. Sara asked him what had caused him to think that she was interested in someone else, and Todd told her that he had seen how she had smiled, flirted, and spent a lot of time with Bart at the party. Sara was stunned. She did not recall treating Bart any differently than anyone else at the party, and she certainly wasn't interested in him. After much explaining and entreating on her part, Todd seemed to accept that she was not trying to dump him.

Todd and Sara continued their relationship for a year, but they finally broke up after several incidents in which Todd became jealous and withdrawn. Sara gave up trying to persuade him that she was not going to leave him for someone else, only to be confronted with the same charge time after time.

Sara and Todd's situation is an example of how jealousy can affect a relationship, and it points to the irrational nature of jealousy. Nothing Sara did or said could persuade Todd that she cared and was not going to leave him. Sara never understood that Todd required constant reassurance of her fidelity to him, that he craved all her attention and admiration, and that he was constantly alert for any sign that she *might* be thinking about abandoning him. The more she tried to say and do to let Todd know that she cared for him, the less convinced he seemed to be. She could not understand why he saw every man with whom she talked as a rival, but she did see that her efforts to make him see otherwise were not working. She finally became tired of trying and gave up. Todd's fear that Sara would leave him was finally realized.

If you are in a relationship with a jealous partner, you can probably identify with many of the actions and feelings Sara experienced. Trying to provide reassurance, seeking to understand what triggered the jealousy, and trying to modify your behavior are common reactions. If you care for your partner and don't get a thrill out of his jealousy (yes, some people do get a thrill out of their partner's jealousy), you try very hard not to do or say anything that could provoke his jealousy, but your attempts are not entirely successful. You may even feel guilty for not being able to prevent his jealous feelings. Or, after a while, you may give up trying to make him believe that you are faithful and become resentful of the accusations. Neither of these responses is helpful for the relationship.

Sara's case, despite her considerable emotional distress, was relatively mild in comparison to other incidences. There are partners who become jealous when their partners even look at or act pleasant to other people, are suspicious of neighbors and other people casually encountered, and may even be jealous of their partner's relationships with family members and friends. Extreme jealousy can lead to physical abuse, and even homicide. These are severe cases with unacceptable outcomes.

How This Book Can Help You

This book is intended to

- help you better understand why your partner gets jealous

- present a framework of how jealousy develops

- describe the roles that narcissistic wounding and narcissistic rage play in jealousy

- identify four styles of jealous behavior

- increase your awareness of your feelings and reactions to your partner's jealousy and how they are beneficial or not beneficial

- describe how the need for affection, attention, power, control, and competition shape the jealous behavior and attitudes, and the resulting reactions

- present alternative internal and external responses to jealousy

The basic premises of the book are that jealousy is not a manifestation of love, and that jealousy is irrational. The seeds of jealousy are planted in childhood and represent a form of insecure attachment—the partner of a jealous person does not "cause" the jealousy. The jealous person fears the loss of the relationship, even when there is no rational reason to believe that will happen.

In this book, care is taken not to put the responsibility for the jealousy on its target, that is, the other partner. You, as the target of jealousy, are not the problem, and this is made clear in the descriptions of the seeds of jealousy, and other possible background experiences. If you are made to feel that you trigger the jealousy, this puts the responsibility and burden on you, the "victim," rather than on the jealous person.

Jealousy can be used as a form of emotional abuse; thus, care is taken in this book to not tell you to avoid doing anything to provoke the jealousy, since this would put you in the "victim" position. However, your behavior and attitudes are examined, because your need for power or competition may lead you to do and say things that get your needs met; but if so, you are meeting your needs at the expense of your partner's fears of being abandoned or destroyed. Therefore, self-examination is an important component in the book.

Finally, alternatives for internal and external responses will be presented. These are put into two categories: constructive and not constructive. You will be guided in reflecting on your behaviors and attitudes to promote personal growth, and to reduce some self-absorbed behaviors and attitudes, such as a need for attention, need for admiration, lack of empathy, and attitude of entitlement.

Chapter 1 defines jealousy and gives a brief overview of the four styles discussed in later chapters and descriptions of four categories of factors related to jealousy.

Chapters 2 through 5 describe in detail the factors that contribute to jealousy. Chapter 2 debunks the myth that *triggers,* something you do or say that causes the other person to become jealous, are to blame for your partner's jealousy. You are not to blame.

Chapter 3 presents some factors that influenced how your inner self developed. Everyone has the same factors, but each of us develops in different ways. This chapter will help you begin to understand your inner self, and your partner's self.

Chapter 4 focuses on past experiences and how they can affect people and their relationships throughout their lives. Chapter 5 presents a discussion of some personal characteristics that can contribute to jealousy.

Four styles of jealousy—clingy, paranoid, manipulative, and exhibitionistic—are described in chapters 6 and 7. You can rate your partner, and yourself, to identify a characteristic jealousy style. Also presented are some possible responses for each style that can help you better cope with the distressing feelings that you may have when confronted with your partner's jealousy.

Chapter 8 summarizes the information presented about jealousy and its various styles and offers strategies for appropriate responding.

Definitions

We probably have all been jealous at some point in our life, and so we can all identify with this feeling. However, few people have an understanding of the roots or causes for their jealousy, and even fewer are able to work on their feelings to reduce or eliminate jealousy. To discover what *jealousy* means to you, let's do an exercise before we look at the formal definition.

Exercise 1: Jealousy

Materials: Two sheets of paper, a pen or pencil, and a set of felt markers or crayons.

Procedure: Find a quiet place to work where you will not be disturbed. Follow the steps as listed.

1. Write the word *jealousy* at the top of one sheet of paper.

2. Write all the thoughts, ideas, words, and phrases that come to mind when you think about jealousy.

3. After you make your list, review it and write a summary statement or paragraph about jealousy.

4. Use the next sheet of paper and your markers to draw some symbolic representations of jealousy and its associations from your list. The symbols can be realistic, abstract, or splotches of color—anything you want.

5. Review all that you have completed. This forms your definition of jealousy.

Dictionary definitions of *jealousy* include the following:

- fear or wariness of being replaced by a rival, especially in regard to another's affection

- vindictiveness toward another because of supposed or actual rivalry

- demanding exclusive worship and love

- fear of losing someone's affection or love

- the suspicion of rivalry or unfaithfulness

Each of the above definitions has either a direct or an indirect expression of fear and personal insecurity. Jealousy seems to include an absence of trust in the other person's ability to remain faithful, and a very definite self-absorption.

Another concept that seems to be a part of the definition of *jealousy* is rivalry, or competition. This adds another dimension, since it brings winning and losing in as a part of the situation. And, every time there are winners and losers, there can be lingering enmity, resentment, rancor, bitterness, and a desire for revenge. Jealousy then becomes more complex and dangerous.

Styles of Jealousy

The four styles of jealousy in relationships are clingy, paranoid, manipulative, and exhibitionistic. These styles are a combination of inner needs, ways of relating and experiencing, and past experiences and how they were internalized. These styles are very complex, and you may find that your partner does not clearly fit any one of them, or that he fits some part of all of them. Although he may not match a particular style, by learning about the various styles you can still gain some understanding and knowledge that will enable you to understand your partner better and develop some effective ways to manage your anxiety and other feelings aroused by your partner's jealousy.

If your partner's jealousy is the *clingy* style, he is very demanding that your time, attention, and interest be given only to him. He is very attentive to you, does nurturing and caring things for you, and takes good care of you. This may sound desirable, and these are some of the behaviors and attitudes that attracted you to him in the first place. However, he also goes overboard with his attentiveness. He can be

- smothering
- overwhelming
- touchy
- picky about trivia and meaningless details
- hurt when you don't tell him your every thought, feeling, and idea
- trying to become "fused" with you

There are certainly degrees of clingy behavior, but you get the picture. Your feelings will tell you if your partner has a clingy style—if you feel overprotected, as if you are suffocating from attention and you cannot be independent as well as interdependent, then you may have a partner with a clingy style.

The *paranoid* style of relating and jealousy is one in which the person sends double messages: get closer, but don't get close. Your partner desperately desires intimacy but is also desperately afraid of it. His family of origin and other past experiences have caused him to mistrust others, to keep them at a distance for fear that he will be hurt and destroyed. He has been deeply disappointed by others in the past, and he expects that you too will deeply disappoint him. He continues to perceive the current relationship with you in terms of his past relationships regardless of all your efforts and considerable evidence to the contrary.

The paranoid style is a very uncomfortable one to live with. Your relationship has a lot of tension, and you may not even realize just how much tension and stress there is. Your partner is

- suspicious and skeptical about people and their motives

- always expecting to be disappointed and is seldom pleased

- very precise, rigid, and controlling

- on the lookout for signs that you don't care for him or are losing interest

- alert to possible threats coming at him from every direction

You may wonder how you were ever attracted to someone like this. He is edgy and tense, expects the worst almost all the time, and cannot be comforted, or at least it seems so. What probably happened is that initially he was able to contain and manage the intensity of his attitudes and feelings and, although you were aware of some of this, you were not aware of just how deep and enduring these attitudes and feelings were. In addition, he probably touched something within you that led you to want to help him understand that not everyone is out to get him, and that you are different. You *are* different, but he cannot let go of his past experiences to be able to relate to you as a different person.

The *manipulative* style is just what it sounds like: sly, deceitful, cunning, and persuasive. You, of course, don't recognize the negative side of his charm at first. You tend to excuse his behavior, think that you misunderstood, and generally see him through rose-colored glasses. Your partner is always finding ways to get you to do what he wants you to do, and you don't understand why you cannot resist his manipulations.

To get an idea of how he manipulates you and everyone else, take a look at the following games he can play. When he plays these games, you end up doing what he wants, even if that something is not in your best interest.

"You are not giving me the attention I want."

"Give me the admiration I crave."

"I don't need you."

"Others need to recognize my superiority."

"Aren't I wonderful!"

Now, he does not ask directly for your attention or admiration. Instead, he seeks these in indirect ways that leave you upset, confused, guilty, and even angry without really understanding why you are feeling the way you do. As long as you continue to experience these uncomfortable feelings, he is able to get you to bend to his will, and he does not need to be open about it. You can't challenge him because there is nothing out in the open, and he can easily deny whatever you say.

The *exhibitionistic* style is the easiest for outsiders to see. Your partner doesn't seem to be hiding anything and stays "on" almost all the time. When you first met, you were probably attracted to the flamboyant behavior and wondered what someone so wonderful saw in you.

Your exhibitionistic partner behaves in ways to get attention and admiration, and as long as you are willing to take second place he is content. He cannot stand anyone outdoing him in anything, and he is very quick to downplay others' attributes, achievements, and possessions. He is concerned about

- having constant attention

- being recognized as unique and special

- the amount of admiration he receives

- others' perceptions that he is deserving and superior

Whenever your partner senses any lessening of your attention and admiration (i.e., you are not giving him your total attention), he becomes upset and worries that you will abandon him. Anything less than total attention is not acceptable to him.

Factors Related to Jealousy

The following table presents the major categories for factors relative to jealousy: immediate, self factors, past experiences, and family of origin. Each will be briefly described below and will receive more in-depth exploration in later chapters.

Factors Related to Jealousy			
Immediate Factors	**Self Factors**	**Past-Experience Factors**	**Family-of-Origin Factors**
Thoughts	Self-efficacy	Support	Mirroring/ empathy
Images	Self-perception	Satisfaction	Parental Destructive Narcissism
Actions	Control	Betrayal	Sibling rivalry
Words	Needs affection	Rejection	Parental rivalry
Clothing	Needs nurturance	Alienation	Parental perceptions
	Needs deference	Shame	Abandonment issues
	Healthy adult narcissism		Destruction issues
	Under-developed narcissism		

Immediate Factors

Immediate factors are the internal triggers for jealousy. Because of the other factors—family of origin, past experiences, and self—they are unique for each person and remain largely unknown to that person. These factors are termed *immediate* because, although the responses to them are internal, something in the present environment sets them off.

Immediate factors are discussed in this book so that you can better understand the futility of your trying to anticipate and deal with them. Your partner's internal responses are an outcome of his personal growth, development, and past experiences. In other words, his triggers, which provoke a fear response, are buried deep in his background and are apt to be set off anytime, anyplace, and with anyone. Everything and everyone can be perceived as a threat to the fearful person, and the more that person rationalizes, denies, and suppresses the fear, the worse it can become.

Self Factors

Self factors are parts of your core, or essential self, that are developed from birth, and that development continues throughout your life. How, and how much, your self develops plays a major role in jealousy.

These are the factors that comprise your psychological self, an inner experiencing and perception of yourself, and of the world. Your self is thought to form as a result of an interaction between your basic personality and temperament (with a strong genetic component), the parental care and nurturing you received, and other environmental experiences you encounter. Your self is very complex, and much of it can be hidden from you and others, but it still exerts influence on your behavior, attitudes, and perceptions.

Examples for some self components are listed in the preceding table, and each of these has other components. For example, healthy adult narcissism includes creativity, empathy, an appropriate sense of humor, wisdom, and so forth. The factors are much too complex to try to explain here, although more explanation is provided in chapter 3.

Suffice it to say that you are born with some parts of some factors, such as a need for affection; your parental care and nurturing helps produce some factors, such as understanding yourself as separate and distinct from others; and environmental experiences contribute to other factors, such as self-efficacy and self-esteem. Further complicating matters is that all your self factors interact with and influence each other, making it difficult to identify a specific one. To better understand your self, and your jealous partner, try to describe some of your self factors and their associations with feelings, especially jealousy.

Self factors contribute to the development of jealousy in many ways. They affect the following:

- sense of personal security and safety

- perceived threats or danger to the self

- the extent and form that the fear of abandonment will take

- perceived ability to effectively care for oneself

- needs for power and control

- faith and trust in others

- strong understanding of the self as distinct and separate from others

- self-identity

It's okay to have jealous feelings; the task then is to manage and contain them so that other people are not affected by your fear, shame, and insecurity, and to accept that these are *your* feelings triggered by your response to a perceived threat. The other person did not cause you to become jealous; you chose to become jealous because of your contributing factors for jealousy.

Past Experiences

Previous relationships also play a major role in the emergence of jealousy. For example, if someone repeatedly reaches out and tries to connect to others to form friendships and intimacy, only to meet with rejection many times, this person will be wary and tentative in establishing other relationships. He will not easily trust others, fearing that they too will reject him, and may tend to be suspicious that others too will find him to be not good enough. He may tend to try and hold others too tightly to ensure that they will remain with him.

On the other hand, a person who experiences supportive and satisfying relationships throughout his life is more trusting and confident. He doesn't live his life on edge, fearing abandonment or rejection. He is able to form and maintain constructive, trusting relationships and is not constantly looking for signs that the other person in the relationship is losing interest, being seduced to leave, or does not care for him. This does not mean that there is an absence of jealousy—it just means that jealousy is not easily triggered and that they are not always on the alert for signs of rejection or betrayal.

Many past experiences can carry "unfinished business": although the experiences or relationships are over, there are still matters and feelings that were left dangling or uncompleted. These matters and feelings are not necessarily on a conscious level, but they do continue to exert their influences on people and their relationships in unconscious ways. A prime example is an unsatisfactory ending of a relationship. Some, or all, of the following could result:

- You don't have a chance to say what you appreciated or liked about the person.

- You just leave and don't say good-bye.

- You feel confused or don't understand something, but you do not have a chance to ask for clarification.

- You continue to carry strong suppressed feelings about the person, or the relationship.

- You intended to show gratitude but failed to take time to do it.

- You experience regrets for your actions, inactions, and other failures or inadequacies.

- You substitute activity, such as going to a party or cleaning the house, to keep from expressing feelings of loss and grief.

The trouble with unfinished business is that you never know when it will emerge and cause trouble, or the form it will take. For example, you can tell yourself that the new person in your life is different, but you may still react to the new person in terms of the old relationship without realizing what you are doing. This can be a part of what is happening with your jealous partner.

Family of Origin Factors

Family of origin factors can contain the seeds of jealousy for adults. Experiences with parents, siblings, and other people close to your family during your formative years can have the following effects:

- establish a sense of personal security

- form a feeling of being worthy and valued
- foster separation and individuation and help you form your own self-identity
- promote the development of strong and resilient boundaries
- help to establish self-efficacy
- are instrumental in developing self-confidence and self-esteem

It is the rare person who cannot see how his family of origin experiences play a major part in how he is today. No matter how much one forgets, denies, rationalizes, or works on those early experiences, they continue to play a major role in the adult's life, reactions, and relationships. Hence, understanding how you came to be as you are is important for your continual growth and development, and that understanding can help you better understand how some family of origin experiences continue to affect your partner.

The seeds of your partner's jealousy were probably planted early, and some circumstances out of the family's control could have contributed. Following are examples of some circumstances that may have been within the family's control, and some that were out of their control:

- birth of a sibling
- divorce
- death of a parent
- job loss
- frequent moves
- parental depression
- severe illness of a family member
- emotional disturbance or mental illness of a parent or sibling
- prison sentence
- military service

The beginnings of jealousy lie in feelings of fear, abandonment, loss, and insecurity that were established early in the person's life. These reasons were not known or adequately addressed at the time, so the person continues to carry them, unconsciously transfers or projects them on their new relationships, and does not adequately resolve them even as an adult.

The jealous person may only know what he feels, with no understanding of why these feelings emerge. The person continues to externalize, or *project,* the cause for the feelings onto others in his world, blaming them for his feelings.

The Psychologically Secure Person

Since insecurity is one of the characteristics that underlie jealousy and you are working to try to understand your jealous partner, you may find it helpful to learn what makes up a psychologically secure person. This person is not perfect by any means but is able to remain centered and grounded regardless of external circumstances. He may become jealous but is able to manage and contain jealous feelings so that they do not poison the relationship. The psychologically secure adult has the following characteristics:

- healthy adult narcissism

- trust in others

- optimism

- ability to feel and express a wide range of emotions

- the understanding that others are separate and distinct individuals

- a strong personal identity

- the ability to be both independent and interdependent

- constructing meaning and purpose in life

- not falling apart under adverse circumstances—the ability to mobilize inner resources to deal with crises

- development and maintenance of meaningful and satisfying relationships

- sociable without fearing being alone

- understanding the need for competition, and the need for cooperation; ability to use both constructively

As you can see, these are internal characteristics that are manifested in the person's behavior. You cannot observe these traits; you can only infer them from what the person says or does.

Information presented in this book will guide you to better understand both yourself and your jealous partner. As you read, just remind yourself that your partner's jealousy is an internal and individualistic feeling that is irrational. You did not cause it. Instead, it is caused by or related to complex experiences your partner has had throughout his life. Indeed, your partner may not even be aware of the factors, experiences, or fears that are causing his jealousy.

Chapter 2

Triggers of Jealousy (Immediate Factors) and Why They Don't Matter

We begin the process of understanding your jealous partner by discussing the immediate factors—the events that can appear to lead to jealousy. These factors are more easily presented and understood than some other factors, since they are observable and don't require inferences or interpretation. But first, let's get some sense of your perception of your partner's jealousy.

when its bad, its really bad. but when we dropit display it its ok

Exercise 2: My Partner's Jealousy

_6_ 1. Rate your partner's jealousy on a scale of 1 to 10, with 1 being little or none, and 10 being extreme or considerable.

_5_ 2. Rate the frequency of your partner's displays of jealousy on a scale of 1 to 10, with 1 as a rating of almost never, and 10 as a rating of almost always.

varies _5-8_ 3. Rate the distress you continually feel because of your partner's jealousy on a scale of 1 to 10. A rating of 1 indicates little or no continual distress, and 10 indicates considerable continual distress.

_5_ 4. Rate the effectiveness of your efforts to prevent or reduce your partner's jealousy on a scale of 1 to 10. A rating of 1 indicates little or no effectiveness, and a rating of 10 indicates that you were extremely effective.

If each of your ratings for items 1 to 3 was below 5, and your rating for item 4 was above 5, then you probably don't think that there is a problem with your partner's jealousy. But if your ratings for items 1 to 3 were each above 5, and your rating for item 4 was below 5, you most likely perceive your partner's jealousy as troubling.

Let's assume that you are distressed. Your partner's behavior troubles you and is negatively affecting the relationship, and you have not yet figured out how to prevent or reduce the displays of jealousy.

One of the first things people generally think about as an antidote to their partner's jealousy is to identify the trigger, or triggers. Triggers are events, behavior, and the like that seem to arouse jealousy. The flawed reasoning goes something like this: once the triggers are identified, then you can do, or not do, that particular thing, and the partner will not become jealous. For the reasonable person who has jealous moments, this might work. For example, if your partner infrequently becomes jealous, but seems to frequently become jealous when your ex-lover calls and talks for some time, you can shorten the amount of time on the phone and recount the reason for the call to your partner when you finish. That might help, or it may not. If you have ever tried to do something about an identified trigger, you probably found that something else took its place and the jealousy remained. This is why a focus on identifying triggers is flawed reasoning.

Let's discuss some possible triggers as listed in the table in chapter 1 under Immediate. These are thoughts, images, actions (and nonverbal behaviors), words, and clothing.

Thoughts

Thoughts are defined as information processing: how you take in data, how you attempt to make sense of it or bestow meaning on the data, and the outcome of this procedure. This is an artificial distinction between thoughts and images, because thoughts can involve images. However, it is easier to separate the two at this point and present them separately.

Thought, as information processing, is one means by which we try to understand our world. We consider thinking a way of being rational, logical, and objective. However, thoughts are also affected by the person's traits and history, including the following:

- personality

- past experiences

- acquired knowledge

- beliefs, attitudes, and values

- innate abilities

- awareness

- attunement to internal and external experiencing

- self-esteem, self-confidence, and self-efficacy

- narcissism, both underdeveloped aspects and developed aspects

Thoughts can also be irrational and imperfect. They are irrational when many of the aspects listed above influence them to process information in such a way that the outcomes do not mesh with reality and are distorted. Thoughts can be imperfect when they try to impose order on, or make sense of, sensory input.

For example, an existing condition such as a sinus infection, or a chronic condition such as a hearing deficit, will affect what a person hears. She may not hear everything someone says, but the brain's information processing fills in the blanks. This imperfect and inaccurate attending and processing is also affected when people translate new experiences according to their old ones, use selective perception, lack valid information, and use other means to try to make sense of what they are seeing, hearing, and internally experiencing.

Irrational Thoughts

Irrational thoughts are generally thoughts about oneself that are not logical, objective, or realistic. They don't break with reality as do delusions, nor do they have the fantasies of illusions. Irrational thoughts are perceptions of the self that are internalized as a result of early interactions with parents, caregivers, and others and, to some extent, are absorbed from the culture. Everyone has some level of irrational or faulty assumptions about what one should be and do, but these can range from mild to severe.

These irrational thoughts influence thinking, feeling, and actions. In many cases the person remains unaware of the irrational nature of their thoughts, and of the negative impact these may have on their relationships and sense of personal well-being.

What are some irrational thoughts a jealous partner may have? The following list presents some examples:

- If my partner pays attention to someone, that signals that he doesn't want me.

- When my partner enjoys the company of someone else, that means that he wants to leave me.

- When my partner says something approving of another person, that means he perceives me as deficient.

- If I were perfect, then my partner would never find anyone else to be attractive (or admirable, good enough, etc.)

- When my partner seems to like someone else, that means that he does not think I am good enough.

- When other women (or men) find my partner to be attractive and personable, that means he is thinking that he can find someone better than me.

- If my partner really loved me, he would never want to be with anyone else, such as family or friends, and would only want to be with me.

- If I were good enough, I would be able to control my partner.

Self-reflection: Could my partner have many of these thoughts?

These are just a few possible irrational thoughts. Included or embedded in these thoughts are feelings of helplessness, a need for power and control over another person, a self-perception of being flawed, and a yearning to feel safe in a relationship. Again, we see that these are internal thoughts, unique to that person, about which an outsider can do nothing.

It is interesting that few, if any, irrational thoughts are changed by experiences. For example, a person who has the irrational thought that she is not good enough will often continue to think so even in the face of considerable evidence to the contrary. This person's successes—having people who love her and enjoy her company, and receiving rewards and approval—will do little to refute her irrational thought about herself. She will continue to search for and focus on clues that she thinks validate the irrational thought that she is not good enough. Thus, every mistake gets exaggerated, she is hypersensitive to any hint of perceived criticism about herself, and she constantly seeks reassurance that she is good enough but never gets enough reassurance. She is also demanding and critical of others, and she blames others for not being perfect.

Imperfect Thoughts

You can expect that your thoughts may be imperfect, since almost everyone experiences this. Impaired sensory input, selective perception, lack of valid information, and perceiving new experiences in terms of old ones can contribute to imperfect and inaccurate thoughts. Whenever your visual, auditory, or other sensory input is impaired, you may not be able to receive complete and accurate information, you may receive distorted input, and you may ignore or overlook important information. Your brain works with what it gets, and if that input is incomplete or inaccurate, then the outcome (your thoughts), is also inaccurate.

People also use selective perception when they consciously or unconsciously attend to certain stimuli in the environment. They decide that some stimuli are important and other stimuli are not. This decision is made on the basis of what is important to that person and is not always logical or rational.

Imperfect thoughts are also caused by lack of valid information, such as, not knowing or understanding systems, processes, or specific information. The thoughts are imperfect because you don't have complete knowledge and understanding, and this can lead to flawed thinking.

Perceiving the New in Terms of the Old

A common thought pattern helps us make sense of what is new and unknown: whenever we encounter something or someone new, it appears that we immediately search for something that is familiar to help with our understanding. It does not matter what or who the new object or person is, our need for understanding pushes us to seek something familiar as a reference point. This tendency is the basis for misunderstandings, misinterpretations, and other errors, especially in relationships.

The following exercise gives you an example of how the old can influence perceptions of the new.

Exercise 3: Old and New

Materials: A sheet of paper, a pen or pencil, and a ruler.

Procedure: Find a private place to complete the exercise where you are unlikely to be disturbed.

1. Draw lines for three vertical columns on the paper.

2. Think of a person in your life, such as your partner.

3. Write the person's name at the top of the first column.

4. Write a list of the person's behaviors, attitudes, beliefs, and other attributes in the first column under the person's name. These can be positive, and/or negative and troubling.

5. Write "Mother" at the top of the second column.

6. Review the list of the first person's characteristics, and in the second column make a check mark for those characteristics that you also see as present in *your* mother.

7. Write "Father" at the top of the third column.

8. Review the list of the first person's characteristics, and in the third column make a check mark for those characteristics that you also see in *your* father.

9. Review all columns and note which characteristics are shared by two or all three people. If you desire, you can identify the characteristics that are also present in you. It is very unlikely that you will find no shared characteristics across the three columns.

This exercise can illustrate how you unconsciously perceive your partner in terms of your parental relationships. People in the mental health field call this *transference* and transference affects relationships without your awareness.

Selective Perception

Another imperfect thought process is selective perception. Everyone tends to select certain stimuli to focus on and respond to as a means of making sense of information being received. What you choose to see, hear, and respond to influences what information is processed, and how it is processed to produce meaning. For example, have you ever responded to a person and then realized that you did not hear or had screened out an important part of that person's message? This has happened to almost everyone.

Selective perception can result when you are

- distracted

- daydreaming

- emotionally intense

- dealing with competing events, people, motives, and so on

- ill or not feeling well

- upset about something that is unrelated to the present

- in touch with your insecure feelings

- searching for, or alert to, hints of blame or criticism

- yearning to have a need fulfilled, such as the need for approval, affection, or acceptance

---

Self-reflection: Do many of these fit me? Do many seem to fit my partner?

Most of these internal reasons for selective perception are unintentional. That is, the person does not consciously decide to be selective because of her condition, such as being emotionally upset. Indeed, the person may not even realize that she is being selective. But these internal states have a powerful influence on what receives the person's attention. Thus, the jealous partner will not see that you spent most of your time at the party with her; she will only see that portion of your time that you spent with someone else. Or, your partner will not hear the politeness in your voice when you speak to someone, she will only note that you spoke to the person and were not hostile and can fill in the blank with the notion that you are attracted to that person.

There are some external influences that increase selective perception, such as noise; a large number of people or things like moving vehicles nearby; an attention-demanding event such as a play; a task one is trying to perform; and alcohol or drug consumption. People cannot pay attention to everything at the same time, especially when their senses are impaired even slightly; therefore, they select what seems to be important to pay attention to at the time.

Physical Conditions or Deficiency

When the senses are impaired by a physical condition, deficiency, or medication, the information sent and received can be incomplete, incorrect, or distorted. This leads to inaccurate data processing, which in turn leads to a flawed output or conclusion. Further, the information processing itself can be affected by the impairment.

When someone cannot see or hear, the condition is easily understood as limiting for information input. This doesn't mean that the person is severely limited, since most people compensate for what is missing, such as one's vision. But when someone has a condition or deficit that is not as apparent, it is not as easily understood. The person may not even be aware that she is impaired with regard to sensory input.

It is impossible to describe all the physical conditions and deficits that can make a difference in our ability to take in and process sensory data. A few can serve as examples:

- a slight hearing loss that the affected person is unaware of

- lack of sleep or restless sleep for a period of time

- interactions between some medications

- side effects of medications

- mixing medications with drugs or alcohol

- some food and medication interactions

- persistent pain

- discomfort caused by a chronic condition

- vertigo, dizziness, and the like

- physical conditions that affect thinking

Impairment can lead to selective perception, distraction by personal concerns, and a flawed thinking process. If you have ever taken medication containing a narcotic for pain, then you have some idea of how your thinking can be impaired. You probably noticed that this medication made it harder to think, caused you to be sleepy, or made you so zonked out that you really didn't want to do much of anything. However, you probably realized what you were experiencing at that time. People with chronic conditions may be so accustomed to living with their physical problem that they (and their companions) are not aware of any impairment.

These conditions and deficits do not have to produce impaired or distorted thinking. What is intended in this discussion is to make you aware of the potential for impaired thinking where there are physical conditions or problems present, either permanent or temporary.

Lack of Valid Information

A lot of trouble and emotional distress is caused by lack of valid information, and jealousy is no exception. Your jealous partner may hear something that arouses her suspicion, may be told about something you allegedly did or said that seems to indicate a loss of attention or affection, or may be the recipient of someone's malicious imaginative thinking. In any of these cases, your partner's reaction is not based on reality, because she does not have complete or valid information. The outcome can be very unpleasant for both of you.

Valid information can be very difficult to obtain, and there are many times when the validity resides in the messenger. That is, you trust the person giving you the information. It is not the same as obtaining information in an investigation, audit, or other evaluation where supporting documentation can be found and produced. In situations involving people's motives, intents, and even alleged actions, there is unlikely to be supporting documentation. And, in this age of digital photography when photographs can be altered, you cannot even rely on the camera for validity and accuracy. Thus, your partner's jealousy can be aroused by hearing an innuendo, a suggestion of impropriety, distortions of real events, gossip, lies, or inferences.

There may be no way to prove what your partner heard or saw, but even more troubling is that there are few effective means for you to refute your partner's allegations. Your partner and you must maintain a reasonable level of trust in each other so that when damaging information is received that cannot be verified, you both reject it because of the trust you have for each other. Trying to disprove hurtful, unverifiable information is futile, consumes energy and time that could be spent in more productive ways, and does not speak to the real issue, lack of trust.

Self-reflection: Have I experienced any of these situations, such as my partner responding to an innuendo? Do I engage in any of these actions, such as gossip?

Filling in the Blanks

One of the most fascinating things about how the brain processes information is its tendency to "fill in the blanks." That occurs when something may not be seen, heard, felt, or smelled but, if the person thinks that it should be present, her information processing adjusts to include it as if it were present. The person is then convinced that it was present, and that her perception is accurate. This is one of the reasons eyewitnesses are notoriously inaccurate.

An example of this is when several witnesses are asked for a description of the offending vehicle in a hit-and-run accident where several people were present. The vehicle may be described as a blue pickup, a red minivan, a green sedan, and a two-tone station wagon. If asked about the vehicle's model, the witnesses may come up with a wide range of answers. Questions about the year of the vehicle may produce even more confusion. Everyone saw the car, but no two saw the same thing. Their brains filled in some of the missing information.

Something similar could happen to trigger jealousy in your partner. For example, suppose you come home with a smudge of lipstick on your cheek. What really happened was that you ran into your mother when you went out to lunch, and she kissed you. You think that you have removed all the lipstick, but there is a little left. Your partner fills in the blank: lipstick mark means you kissed another woman. If your partner's jealousy were not easily triggered, she might just point out the lipstick and you could simply recount what happened. On the other hand, if the situation did trigger her jealousy, you might find yourself in a fight without realizing what happened, or she might give you the silent treatment.

The discussion up to this point has focused on thoughts and how they can trigger jealousy, the differences in the ways people take in and process information, and how thoughts can incorporate faulty reasoning. We now turn to the other immediate components of immediate factors: images, actions, words, and clothing.

Images

Images are visualizations that occur in the mind. We don't have a clear idea of where these come from, but they are powerful contributors to our thinking. Images can also fuel our fantasies and imagination, assist in problem solving, provide guidance and direction, and give encouragement and support. Images can come from real events, as in a memory or flashback of a certain event, or they can be a fantasy, such as a daydream. Some people are very aware of what images are real for them and which are not, while other people get confused and believe that their fantasies are real. These are not delusions or hallucinations, which are associated with mental disturbances, reactions to some medications, or the result of ingesting controlled substances. These images just seem so real that the person can begin to believe in their reality.

Images and dreams differ in that imagining occurs while you are awake, and dreams happen during sleep. For most people, their dreams just emerge without direction or guidance on their part. Images, on the other hand, can be guided and directed by you on the conscious level. A good example of this is when you image what you will do when you win the lottery. You can image what you want to do with the money, how you will act when you receive the news that you won, and what you will buy or do first with the winnings. You can have a really good time directing your images about this.

There are also some similarities between dreams and images. Both can involve symbols that have meaning for the person; sometimes these are unwanted intrusive visualizations that emerge; they are not always pleasant; and it can be difficult to let go of their affect, and of the visualization itself. These can be more troubling for the individual when the images occur during waking hours, since there can be a belief or assumption that you have more control over your images than you do over your dreams. For many people this is true, and a dose of realistic thinking can help dismiss the troubling image. However, some people cannot let go, and the more they try to let go, the more troubling the image becomes. They can try to repress and deny the image and its emotional impact, but that doesn't work either. If the person continues to think about that image, the line between its unreality and reality can become blurred, and the person can begin to believe that the image is real.

The situation described above is what can happen in a jealous partner. An image emerges in her mind, she tries to reject it but is unsuccessful, the image persists, and it becomes real for her. These images can emerge at any time and under any condition or circumstance and do not need an incident to trigger them. Once they emerge, the person is not able to control them. The images that trigger jealousy can result from the following:

- past experiences

- fear of abandonment

- attempts to get reassurance that she is loved and cared for

- basic insecurity

- lack of trust

- fears of personal inadequacy

As you can see, the images arise from factors and forces within that person and are not external. Yes, you can see or hear something that gets your imagination off and running, but the images and their direction are internal and unique to the person.

To get some idea of the power of images, complete the following exercise.

Exercise 4: A Growing Plant

Materials: Several sheets of unlined paper, a pen or pencil, and a set of colored felt markers or crayons.

Procedure: Find a quiet place to work where you will not be disturbed. Complete each of the following steps, one at a time. Finish one step before moving on to the next one.

1. Close your eyes and imagine that you are selecting a plant. This can be a flower, shrub, tree, or whatever you choose. The plant is young and just beginning to emerge from the soil. When you are ready, open your eyes and draw your young plant.

2. Close your eyes and visualize your plant after you got it home—you have repotted or planted it in your yard and it has been growing for a month or more. Open your eyes and draw your plant at this stage.

3. Close your eyes once more and visualize your plant as fully mature. See its beauty, colors, and shape. Once the image is established in your mind, open your eyes and draw your mature plant.

4. Spread your drawings out so that you can see all three at the same time. Use another sheet of paper and write a story or paragraph about your plant and its growth.

5. Look at all you've completed, and reflect on what parallels to your life the plants and story or paragraph represent (for example, your choice of plant, where you planted it, how it looked at different stages, and how it looked when it matured).

Actions and Nonverbal Behaviors

Actions and nonverbal behaviors by or toward other people, such as the following, can trigger jealousy in one's partner:

- displays of affections from mild, such as a pat on the shoulder, to intense, such as kissing

- sitting close to someone, especially when there is more space available

- talking to someone, especially when you appear to be intensely interested

- maintaining eye contact

- touching a person in a fond or intimate way

- trying to spend time with someone

- turning your body so that you are oriented to the person (conveys interest)

- holding hands, giving hugs, and the like

- using a soft, intimate voice tone when talking

- leaning forward (conveys interest and acceptance)

- making gestures that show caring

Self-reflection: Do I deliberately act in any of these ways to try to get my partner's attention?

Actions and nonverbal behaviors toward another person, or that you tolerate from another person, can trigger jealousy because of their similarities and associations to your behavior with your partner. These include signals of intimacy, caring, concern, love, and so on. Your partner may not be able to distinguish between your characteristic behavior with others whom you care about, such as family and friends, and your behavior with her. She may think in global and all-inclusive terms, such as *always, never, all,* and *none,* and not be able to conceptualize in gradations and specific terms such as *sometimes* and *somewhat.* If fear related to power and control are added to this global and all-inclusive thinking, then your partner cannot see your behavior with others as different from your behavior with her. For example, a kiss on her cheek signals your intimacy with and love for her, and when you kiss anyone else on the cheek, she interprets that action as a signal that you are intimate or in love with that person.

You may want to reflect on your actions and nonverbal behaviors that evoke jealous comments from your partner. This is not intended to suggest that you should stop doing what you are doing. Rather, it could be helpful to reflect on your motives for engaging in these behaviors. They may reflect who you are, such as giving hugs to family and friends, but they may have a less-constructive motive, such as getting attention from your partner, or trying to get your partner's reassurance that she cares for you. The fact that the triggered jealousy is your partner's responsibility does not take away your responsibility for your acts that are intended to provoke a jealous reaction; these are actions and behaviors that you will want to consider changing.

You may also want to think about changing any nonverbal behaviors that are sending signals that are unintended or could be misinterpreted by the recipient: it is possible to be friendly without being seductive. You may get a thrill from acting seductive, and from the expression of interest it generates, but is that thrill worth the damage it does to your partner's self-esteem, and to the relationship? Additionally, if you have a motive of revenge because you are angry with your partner, this too needs examination and reflection. The outcome of your actions may not be what you intended, or worth losing the relationship. You are the only one who can make this judgment.

Words

Words can trigger jealousy by evoking images, bypassing defenses, and inflicting narcissistic wounds, which are injuries to the person's essential self (see chapter 5). You cannot know which words or comments, spoken under which circumstances, will wound and allow jealousy to emerge. Your partner herself may not be able to tell you what words are guaranteed to set her jealousy off. Indeed, the same words used under different circumstances can elicit different responses and different reactions.

As noted before, images are very powerful influences on thinking, and they are not always under the person's control. Certain words, when spoken, may evoke images in a person's mind that are unwelcome, uncomfortable, and difficult to dismiss. You can never be sure what words will uncover buried associations with past experiences and feelings. To get a feel for how this happens, try the following exercise.

Exercise 5: Associations

Materials: A sheet of paper and a pen or pencil.

Procedure: Find a quiet place to work where you will not be disturbed.

1. Write the following list of words in a vertical column on one side of the paper: garden, weeds, flowers, birds, sad, sun, grass, yellow, sprinkler, and pleasant.

2. As quickly as possible, write an image or association for each word *in the order it appears.* Don't skip a word, and don't think about the image; just write whatever pops into your mind. It is helpful to not evaluate, edit, or change your first thought.

3. Look at the list of images and associations you have generated. Now, write a sentence about yourself that includes the image or association. Try to stay away from "I like" and "I don't like." Focus on your inner experiencing, past and present relationships, and your hopes, wishes, dreams, and the like. For example, if an association for *weeds* was *tough,* you might write a statement about yourself such as "I can be tough when it is necessary."

4. Read your sentences and associations. Write a summary statement about what your associations evoked for you.

When you are in an intimate relationship you tend to let your guard down, setting aside your defenses and emotional shielding so that you can be accessible to your partner. You let more of your real self be seen since this promotes connections that are meaningful. This is a beneficial aspect of a supportive relationship. However, this openness also puts you in a position where, knowingly or unknowingly, your partner's words can bypass your defenses and tap into your feelings and fears about yourself. The same is true for your partner, and this is why words can be so powerful in evoking jealousy.

Defenses, psychological constructs that we use to keep certain knowledge about ourselves out of our consciousness, ward off feelings of shame and guilt about self, including the following:

- fears of abandonment

- personal inadequacies and flaws (not being good enough)

- not living up to one's expectations for oneself

- the extent of one's self-absorption

By using defenses, we can keep this knowledge hidden from ourselves. As long as we don't know it, or remain unaware of it, we don't have to experience the very painful feelings associated with whatever it is. We also use these defenses to keep others away from this painful material. Examples of defenses and their behavioral manifestations are offered in the table below.

Defense	Behavior
Intellectualization	talks about feelings, events, or people with detachment; focuses on facts
Rationalization	makes excuses for acts, failures, and the like
Repression	stuffs painful or uncomfortable feelings or events instead of working through them
Overcompensation	goes to extremes to achieve, acquire, and act; does too much for others

Defenses are used to prevent narcissistic wounding where shame and guilt feelings are triggered over real, or imagined, personal deficiencies. The person's core, or essential self, is under attack, and the threat must be battled. These wounds go to a deep, and mostly unknown, part of the self that was developed (or not developed) early in life. Some wounds are nicks and can easily be ignored, dismissed, or denied. Others are more hurtful and inflict considerable pain around the person's self-perception, self-efficacy, and self-esteem.

Let's go back to the personal deficiencies, real or imagined, that are feared. These are internalized parental messages about one's worth and value that were transmitted from birth on. These messages were incorporated as part of the self and are an important component of one's self-concept. How your parents perceived you was taken into your self, and both the perception and taking in occurred on the unconscious level. As an infant, you were in the preverbal stage and did not have words for identifying these messages, and they remain unidentified in words even today. We don't know how to access and express these messages that were received and incorporated at the preverbal level. Nevertheless, they continue to exert a real and powerful influence on your self-perception, self-esteem, and self-confidence.

Thus, when your jealous partner is narcissistically wounded, she is most likely reacting to words that evoke feelings of shame over perceived personal deficiencies internalized when she was a child. She may feel defective, inadequate, not good enough, fatally flawed, unable to meet expectations, and unable to "fix" herself.

These states and feelings are painful, and she may react to them by withdrawing or attacking to defend her core self against destruction. As you can see, this process is very complex, and uniquely different for each person. You cannot understand the precise workings of the process in your partner, just as she doesn't understand much or any of it, and just as you do not fully understand the process in yourself. The meanings of words reside within the individual.

Clothing

Does how you dress signal your availability? No, it does not— except in some people's minds, and this is distorted thinking. Signals of availability are in the minds of the receiver, and that is often their fantasy.

However, clothing choices can convey a message that is interpreted by the other person as

- a desire for attention or admiration

- a wish to be thought of as unique and special

- attention to one's self-care

- pride in one's looks and attractiveness

- a need to be trendy or fashionable

After all, there are books and other materials written about dressing to be successful in the work world, how to dress for professional positions, and other such topics. Clothing can actually say quite a lot about who the person is, and it can sometimes carry a specific message.

Your jealous partner may object to your clothing and use the excuse that you are sending the wrong signals with how you dress. What she is really saying is that she is attracted to you in part because of what you wear and likes what she sees, but that she fears that others will also be attracted and woo you away. A common occurrence is for a partner to object to clothing that is exactly the same as or similar to what you wore when she became connected to you. Now, your wearing these clothes is no longer acceptable to her.

The actions of other people can also contribute to the partner's distress and fears. The following kinds of comments and behaviors by others can be upsetting to a jealous partner:

- compliments and comments about body parts, such as how well you fit into those jeans

- whistles and other sounds of approval

- intent gazing at body parts, such as his legs in shorts

- comments about wishing you were available because you look so good

- statements that what you are wearing is a turn-on

These are the kinds of words and actions that can trigger jealous images and thoughts. You cannot prevent your partner from having these thoughts, and you do not cause them by your clothing. However, you may intend to attract attention by what you are wearing to that party, for example. And, your intent may be to remind your partner of your attractiveness by getting this attention. But what you may not take into consideration when you do this is that your partner may become jealous and blame or chastise you for drawing this attention.

Triggers Don't Matter

Triggers are internal personal states for your partner, and your behavior does not cause her jealousy. Some behaviors discussed in this chapter may have associations with your partner's jealousy, and you may want to modify them where possible. But, for the most part, there is little or nothing you can do to eliminate jealousy from emerging. The jealousy is within that person, is related to her inner experiencing, both known and unknown to her, is basically a deepseated fear of abandonment, signals a lack of power and control to her, and is not rational.

Chapter 3

Why Your Partner Turns Green: Some Self Factors

To deepen your understanding of your jealous partner, let's look at some possible ways his inner self could have developed. You must remember that you are an external observer drawing inferences about another person's inner experiencing, and you cannot determine the accuracy of your inferences. There are tests and other assessment techniques that are much more valid, but they too have their flaws. It is not helpful, nor is it constructive, to think of your inferences as facts.

In the table in chapter 1, we listed the following self factors, the factors that define you as a person:

- self-efficacy
- self-perception
- control
- need for affection
- need for nurturance
- need for deference
- healthy adult narcissism
- underdeveloped narcissism

Almost all these topics are the subject of numerous books and articles, and you are encouraged to seek out those on topics of interest to you for more in-depth coverage. This chapter will define each concept, associate it with jealousy, and show you how you can understand it as it relates to you. Of course, the concepts discussed here are not the only self factors you have; I present just a few to give you some notion of just how complex jealousy can be, and why it is so difficult to change it in another person.

Self-Efficacy

Efficacy refers to personal effectiveness, the capacity to produce the desired result, and the ability to achieve results. Embedded in the definition of *self-efficacy* are the following thoughts and feelings about oneself:

- personal adequacy
- proven capability, or the potential for it
- assurance that one can cause something to happen
- ability to influence outcomes
- skillful management
- technical expertise

Thus, self-efficacy is your belief in your ability in all of these qualities. For example, do you believe that you have the intelligence and talent to be successful in your chosen career, or in an intimate relationship? In other words, can you effect the desired results?

As you go through life, your ability to exert influence over what happens to you provides you with evidence about your effectiveness at producing the desired results—your self-efficacy—and you internalize this perception of your effectiveness as part of your belief system about yourself. If you have enough successes at achieving the desired result, whatever that may be, you develop a strong belief in your self-efficacy. If you meet with disappointments often enough, you doubt that your self-efficacy is sufficient. Notice that vague terms, such as *enough* and *often enough,* are used here. That's because there are individual differences between people, since what is enough for one person may not be enough for someone else.

There are many early-life events that could produce doubt about one's self-efficacy:

- frequent moves
- unstable or chaotic family life

- homelessness
- poverty
- extended illness of self or of a family member
- absence of one or both parents
- physical abuse
- emotional abuse
- sexual abuse
- isolation of family (no social support system)
- divorce
- substance abuse in the family
- family violence

Some children develop their sense of self-efficacy despite less-than-desirable events and circumstances. However, some people are left with a deep conviction that they cannot influence what happens to them, be personally effective, or have desirable outcomes. These people usually did not develop a major component for positive self-confidence and will use ineffective means to try to have influence and feel competent. People such as these can be described as bullies, sneaks, cheaters, and manipulators. They may mistrust their ability to hold on to their partners. Their rage over their personal ineffectiveness gets displaced on their partners. Neither person in the relationship can know when the feeling of lack of self-efficacy will emerge, or what will cause it to emerge. This is a part of the self that may be mostly hidden or not understood.

Self-Perception

In his book, *The Emerging Self* (1993), James Masterson describes a healthy self-image, or self-perception, as one where the person thinks and feels about himself as "being adequate, competent, based on reality with some input from fantasy." The person's inner representation of the self is an integrated one that is able to hold both good and undesirable or unwanted aspects of the self at the same time. This means that the person is

- self-accepting
- aware of personal flaws and other imperfections

- confident in his abilities to affect his world in needed ways

- forgiving of his mistakes and errors

- believes that he will survive if left alone to fend for himself

- able to tolerate shame and guilt without falling apart or repressing or denying them

- aware of his self as distinct and separate from others

- primarily realistic

The term *self-esteem* means the extent to which one has a favorable self-perception. Low self-esteem equates with a very unfavorable perception of self, high self-esteem equates with a healthy perception of self, and excessive self-esteem equates with an inflated perception of self.

Exercise 6: Self-Perception Scale

Use the following exercise will help you rate your own self-perception and make inferences about your partner's self-perception. Use the following scale:

5—always, almost always

4—frequently, much of the time

3—sometimes

2—seldom

1—never, or almost never

Me   Partner

_____ _____   1. I feel profoundly ashamed of myself.

_____ _____   2. I find it hard to forgive myself, or cannot forgive myself.

_____ _____   3. When I make a mistake, I feel very bad.

_____ _____   4. I feel flawed and unwanted.

_____ _____   5. I maintain a facade of adequacy, but I really feel inadequate.

_____ _____   6. I cannot get most of my needs met.

_____ _____   7. I feel I am unable to influence others to care for me.

_____ _____   8. I am afraid that others will see me as I really am and will reject me.

_____ _____   9. I don't get enough reassurance of my worth from others.

_____ _____   10. I am disappointed in myself.

Add your ratings to obtain a total score for yourself. Scores ranging from 41 to 50 indicate a very negative self-perception; scores of 31 to 40 indicate a negative self-perception; scores of 21 to 30 indicate some negativity about yourself; scores of 11 to 20 indicate little negativity in your self-perception; and scores of 0 to 10 indicate a high and positive self-perception.

You may not have been able to rate your partner on all items, and so we will use a different scoring procedure for your partner. Count the number of items you rated as 3 or above. Five or more items rated as 3+ indicate a very negative self-perception; three or four items rated as 3+ indicate a negative self-perception; and fewer than three items rated as 3+ may suggest a positive self-perception if you were able to rate your partner on six or more items. If fewer than six items were rated, your rating of your partner's self-perception is inconclusive. However, you may have gained enough information about your partner to understand a little more about his perception of himself.

When your partner does not perceive himself as adequate or competent in a realistic way, that can play a role in triggering his jealousy. These feelings about himself may be buried deep and may not be in his conscious awareness, but they still exert an influence in unconscious ways. A negative self-perception and low self-esteem contribute to his feelings about being effective, worthwhile, and good enough, and these can lead to irrational thoughts about his partner. After all, if you could see him as he sees himself, you too might be as unaccepting of him as he is of himself.

Control

Although it may not seem like it, people who try to control others are really attempting to control themselves. They feel they must have order, influence over others, and power if they are to survive and feel safe. Their world is one of insecurity, uncertainty, and danger to the self. They fear that their self will not be able to exist if they cannot control everything around them. Internal states in controlling behavior include the following:

- a need for certainty

- a need for reduction or elimination of ambiguity

- the desire for reassurance that the self can survive

- a yearning for the conviction that one is competent and capable

- some measure of omnipotence and grandiosity about personal responsibility

- a constant feeling of danger and insecurity

To a person who feels the need to control others, the world is full of hostile forces bent on destroying him, and it is only through his efforts that these forces can be thwarted and the self can survive. These forces are both external and internal, and they operate on the psychic level. There may be real danger in the person's world, but the discussion here focuses on psychic dangers—potential, real, and fantasized.

Everyone can appreciate having some order, predictability, and rationality in their lives. Although you may want some excitement, novelty, and surprises, you don't want a constant dose of these. Living in such situations produces considerable stress, and that takes a toll on your physical, psychological, and emotional self. You stay in an enduring state of tension so that you can be prepared to cope with, repel, or fight whatever comes your way. Examples of extreme circumstances include the following:

- war experience

- prison sentence

- living with a substance abuser

- addiction (yours or that of someone living with you)

- physical abuse
- family violence
- sexual abuse
- emotional abuse
- neglect

The person who has experienced any of these during his lifetime stays uneasy and unsure of when and how he will be hurt or destroyed but is very much aware of the possibility.

Circumstances can be less extreme and less debilitating but nevertheless still produce an environment where the unexpected is the norm. Examples of these include

- insecure employment of one or more parents
- parental depression
- marital discord
- poverty
- living in a neighborhood that is not safe
- an emotionally disturbed family member
- divorce, especially where it is not amicable
- chaotic family life

If your jealous partner experienced one or more of these as he was growing up, he may have a deep-seated and strong need for control in his world so that he can feel safe. This need extends to other people and their behavior. He is not aware of just how deep the need is, or its roots; he is just trying to feel safe and secure. Because his need is on the unconscious level, his unawareness of it means that he does not understand it, cannot manage and contain it, and may use ineffective ways to try to get the need for control met. The need exerts a powerful influence on his feelings, behavior, attitudes, and expectations and extends to everything in his life.

Insufficient psychological boundary strength can also play an important role in the strong attempts to control others. When a person has not developed sufficient psychological boundary understanding, he can have an incomplete sense of where he ends and where others begin. He can see other people as extensions of himself, and as under his control. He cannot perceive anyone else as a separate and distinct person who is independent and autonomous. He is also unaware of this perception and cannot imagine that there are other ways of perceiving self and others. Lack of boundary strength, and perceptions of others as extensions of self, are discussed further in the section on underdeveloped narcissism, and in chapter 5 on family of origin factors.

Need for Affection

All humans seem to have a need for affection. They want to feel that they are valued and cared for and are liked by other people. They need the experience of warmth and tenderness from others.

Affection is not as intense, deep, or passionate as love is. It is calmer, milder, and with more gradations than love has, but it still provides psychological encouragement and support. However, as the recipient of affection, you have to trust that the giver is genuine in his feeling of affection for you. Your jealous partner, however, may have difficulty trusting that other people are genuine.

Another difficulty is when a person did not get the affection he needed early in life and now, as an adult, cannot get enough affection or cannot trust that others will meet this need. This early deprivation sets the stage for adult behavior and feelings of mistrust and longing. The two states clash and keep the person in a state of constant tension, as he reaches out for the desired affection and withdraws from or rejects it because he does not trust it to be genuine. This is very sad, because this person tends to push away the very thing he desires.

Whether your jealous partner's need for affection is influenced by past experiences, family of origin experiences, or a combination of both, the result is that he does not trust that your affection for him is real and enduring. He fears that, since other people in his life did not find him worthy of affection, you also do not find him worthy. The deep, disappointing life experiences cannot be shaken off, and the dread of once more being disappointed is severe even if it is on a nonconscious level (just below the level of awareness but still accessible).

People who are personally secure and grounded do not react to disappointment in relationships the same way as do people who are insecure and not well grounded. They too have a need for affection, but they also trust and believe that their self-worth is sufficient to attract genuine affection. Thus, when they have disappointing relationships, they do not generalize to their other relationships or expect that all their relationships will be disappointing. They can accept that this one did not work out. They may be sad and disappointed, but they still believe that they are good enough to get their need for affection met. They also tend to be accepting of the affection they do receive, and do not become bottomless pits where they cannot get sufficient affection.

Your partner may be the kind of person who gives conditional affection. That is, he gives affection with conditions or strings attached. You will receive his affection only when you can meet his conditions for giving it. Since he has no idea he is doing this, and you cannot read his mind, neither of you may know what these conditions are. This is a highly ambiguous situation, and there is no way to make it clearer. Asking him is futile, since he lacks the needed awareness to be able to articulate it. Gaining enough understanding of him to be able to read his mind is also impossible. If, or when, you are able to meet his conditions, it is only due to luck or happenstance. This makes for a very uncomfortable, edgy, and tension-filled relationship.

To further complicate your relationship, he may feel threatened when you show affection for anyone else; he fears that this means there is less affection for him, or that your affections are being seduced or given away, and that means that you will leave him. His fear of these dreaded events can be triggered by observing you doing any of the following:

- smiling fondly at someone else

- speaking words of approval and fondness for someone

- attending to a person, even in a social situation where this is your responsibility

- showing care and concern about a person's welfare or well-being

- acting in a warm, friendly, and open manner toward someone

- forgiving errors and mistakes others make

- spending time with someone

These and other signs of affection toward anyone in your life, such as family and friends, are perceived as threats by your jealous partner.

Need for Nurturance

Nurturance is also a universal need. Whereas the need for affection is a desire or yearning to be loved and approved of, the need for nurturing focuses on a more basic need that is tied to survival. Everyone needs to be cared for in order to survive. Babies are totally dependent on others for nurturing, while adults are expected to be somewhat self-nurturing and not as dependent on others for their survival. Again, there is the specter of destruction embedded in the need for nurturance. This need is deep-seated and can be unconscious if the person lacks awareness of its intensity and impact.

Although your jealous partner may be capable of fending for himself and can survive, he may also carry a fear of not being cared for, and for him that means he will not be able to survive. People like this can be very dependent and clingy without understanding why they are this way. The objective and rational reality is that they can and do take care of themselves, but they are emotionally and psychologically convinced of their inability to do so.

Adults who did not get their early nurturing needs met, those who received inconsistent or interrupted nurturing, and those who carry old parental messages about their inadequacy can exhibit behaviors like the ones below. Check to see how many of these apply to your partner. If he has five or more, he may have a strong need for nurturing:

- a need for reassurance

- helplessness

- frequent requests to others for assistance or rescuing

- procrastination for fear of being wrong or inadequate

- a strong desire to please others so that they will not abandon him

- frequent checking in with others just to maintain contact

- anxiety when you are away or just out of sight

- a strong desire to be involved in almost everything you do

- looks to you to do things for him that he could do for himself

- clinginess

- wants all of your attention

A person with many of the characteristics listed above can easily become jealous and frequently does so because of this deepseated need for nurturance that is more expected in a child than it is in an adult. You may have been unaware of the extent and depth of his need for nurturing and were not expecting the jealousy. You may stay in a constant state of tension because the jealousy is so frequent, and there seems to be no rhyme or reason for its emergence. Chapter 7 discusses the clingy jealous partner in more detail.

Need for Deference

Deference is the act of showing submission to someone. Although the submission is voluntary and courteous, it also carries the notion that the other person's opinion, wish, or judgment is better in some way. The deferential person is yielding to a superior intellect, status, need, or argument. The person who receives deferential treatment is treated as superior and deserving of the yielding others give him.

The word *deference* has "to defer" as its base, which can simply mean "to put off." There are times and situations where you will want to put off or delay your needs, opinions, judgments, and so on in favor of someone else's needs. The ability to delay gratification is a characteristic of mature adult behavior. Delaying the satisfaction of your needs, not expressing your opinion, and yielding to someone's judgment may be appropriate in many situations. So, to show deference is not undesirable, nor is wanting to be shown deference undesirable in and of itself.

However, if your jealous partner has a strong need for deference, he can become enraged when he does not get it, when you show deference to someone else, or when you refuse to yield and insist on your needs being met. He sees your deference to others as undermining him, a signal that he is inferior in your eyes, which arouses the fear that his hidden inadequacies are revealed, and the thought that you will abandon him is triggered.

The person who has an extreme need for deference can display some of the following behaviors and attitudes:

- becomes upset when someone suggests that he is wrong, or that he made an error

- expects to have his opinions, decisions, and suggestions accepted promptly, without modification or disagreement

- tends to get upset when he feels he does not get the respect he feels he merits

- feels that others should recognize and respect his superior knowledge, ability, intelligence, and the like

- overreacts to perceived opposition for even the smallest thing

- is quick to point out that others would not fail or make errors if they would do what he tells them to do

- does not seem to recognize the validity of others' positions, opinions, and judgments

- has an attitude that his perspective is the only correct one

This extreme need for deference is related to an underlying conviction of personal inadequacy and flaws that is masked by arrogance, grandiosity, and contempt. Thus, when you react to the latter, you are ignoring the hidden thoughts about personal adequacy, and these are the more powerful ones. More is presented on this topic in the section on underdeveloped narcissism in this chapter, and in chapter 8.

Healthy Adult Narcissism: The Developed Self

At first glance, this topic would seem to be out of place here, where the focus is on self factors that underlie jealousy. However, it is discussed so that you can better picture the adult behavior and attitudes that are desirable. We've discussed how some underdeveloped self factors are exhibited, and we now turn to describing what a more cohesive, fully developed self looks like. This is called healthy adult narcissism, and it includes a self-reflective self-focus rather than the self-absorbed one. This fully developed healthy adult narcissism allows you to have better and more satisfying relationships, and to not experience distressing emotions, such as jealousy, as often. You are able to be more rational about yourself, and about others. You also develop the inner resources that help you better cope with your partner's jealousy. This is a very brief presentation that does not provide a full understanding of the concept, it but can serve as an introduction. The aspects of healthy adult narcissism that are presented here are empathy, creativity, an appropriate sense of humor, acceptance of personal responsibility, and a self-reflective stance.

Empathy occurs when you can deeply feel what another person is feeling without losing your sense of being separate from that person. You do not become lost, overwhelmed, or enmeshed with that person's feelings; you are able to feel what he feels for a period of time but are able to pull away at any time. Further, because you maintain your sense of self as separate and distinct, you do not carry the other person's feelings with you when you leave. If you do become lost, overwhelmed, or enmeshed, this indicates insufficient boundary strength, and an incomplete understanding of where you end and where others begin. The adult who can be empathetic has strong and resilient boundaries, does not view others as extensions of himself, and recognizes that he is a separate and distinct person.

The value of empathy cannot be overstated. It is the means by which we convey to others our deep understanding of what they are experiencing, and to receive empathy is very rewarding and validating. It is not often that we are understood on a deep level, and a lack of understanding (and being understood) contributes to feelings of isolation, alienation, not being connected to others in meaningful ways, and even self-doubt.

Creativity is defined as a new, novel, original approach to processes, procedures, products, and so on. While artistic talent contributes to creativity, it is by no means the only indicator and contributor for creativity. You can be creative in any and all parts of your life. For example, you are being creative when you develop a new use for something old, try different ingredients in an usual recipe, plan and plant a garden around a concept or theme, do something new to accomplish a routine task, make up a bedtime story for a child, use existing components to make something new, or improve a thing, product, or process.

If you have artistic talent, you can also be creative in a variety of ways; it just calls for you to find new ways to express your feelings, concepts, and ideas while using your talents.

The value of creativity and the reason that it is a part of healthy adult narcissism is that it requires you to look beyond yourself and to be open to external influences in a reflective and discriminating way. Becoming less self-absorbed and more open in a selective way demands maturity, a strong self-identity, and a willingness to explore and take calculated risks. After all, when you are searching for or trying something new, that involves some risk of failure. A person who refuses to try for fear of failure is not open and is somewhat self-absorbed.

Laughter is good for the body, mind, spirit, and emotions. An *appropriate sense of humor* is also valuable and is thought to be a characteristic of healthy adult narcissism. Healthy adult narcissism allows a person to perceive humor in silly things and life's absurdities, and it means that you can laugh at yourself. This sense of humor does not find amusement in situations or acts that demean or devalue others or attempt to show their inferiority, such as stereotypes, biases, and prejudices; other people's distress, disabilities, or frailties; ethnic, racial, or religious differences; other people's loss of dignity and any acts that seek to undermine a person; one-upmanship, put-downs, and the like; and vulgarity and profanity.

What are humorous are those things that delight, reflect dissonance and inconsistencies, demand that you think, and demonstrate your self-acceptance.

What does this mean for a person with healthy adult narcissism? It means that you

- do not have to see others as inferior in order for you to feel adequate

- are accepting of diversity however it is manifested

- are not focused on a need to be superior

- have empathy and sympathy for those who suffer unfortunate circumstances

- respect gender, age, and other differences and accept these as worthwhile

- are reflective and thoughtful

- are accepting of yourself, flaws and all

Acceptance of personal responsibility has two major components: you recognize your obligations and you are able to let others have their obligations. That is, you have strong and resilient boundaries that help you accept what is your responsibility, and not take on others' responsibilities. This is very important when it comes to feelings, since some people who take on too much personal responsibility can think that they cause other's feelings, have a responsibility to take care of other's feelings, are wrong to allow other people to feel distress or discomfort, or must ensure that harmony is maintained.

There are also people who blame others for what they feel, and this shows a lack of acceptance of personal responsibility. You, and you alone, are responsible for what you feel. Yes, others may say or do something that triggers these feelings, but it is your past experiences and other self factors that cause the feelings, not the other person. This concept can be difficult to accept as it is much more self-affirming to be able to blame someone else for your feelings than having to take on that responsibility—if your feelings are your responsibility, it follows that you are the one who has to take care of them, and that can be a daunting task.

A *self-reflective stance* is one where you are willing and able to engage in self-examination instead of becoming defensive, or attacking. You are psychologically secure enough that you can look at your behavior, attitudes, values, feelings, beliefs, and thoughts to determine their effectiveness, whether they represent the person you want to be, and their impact on your relationships. You do not evade the discomfort that can surround the self-examination, but neither do you become mired in it. The self-reflective person

- is less defensive
- recognizes that there are masked and hidden parts of the self
- may be apprehensive but does not fear self-examination
- is accepting of unlikable parts of himself
- is willing to consider another's comments, opinions, and reactions as valid for that person
- does not have to be correct or right all of the time
- can forgive himself when he is wrong or inadequate

The self-reflective person pays attention to both internal experiencing and communication and feedback from others and can balance them. That is, neither is thought to be totally valid, but looked at together they can be more revealing. An example of self-reflection is when someone becomes jealous, asks himself what triggered this reaction, becomes self-reflective about the reasonableness and rationality of the jealousy, and tries to understand why he feels mistrustful and inadequate. Notice that a shift takes place from the external to the internal and personal. There is no blaming of self or others, just a reflection about his personal reaction and its roots.

Underdeveloped Narcissism

Attaining age-appropriate and healthy adult narcissism is a process that begins at birth and continues throughout one's life. It is thought by some theorists that the care, nurturing, and other experiences one has early in life contribute significantly to the development of the self, and to the parts of self that do not develop along expected lines or in a timely fashion. This topic is much too involved and complex to present in full here; what is addressed are some examples of underdeveloped narcissism as it could relate to your partner's jealousy. You may find it helpful to review the description of healthy adult narcissism as contrasted with that of underdeveloped narcissism. Other points to keep in mind are that the person who has underdeveloped narcissism is totally unaware of the lack of development, and that you too may have some underdeveloped narcissism of which you remain unaware. Presented here are four of many behaviors and attitudes reflective of underdeveloped narcissism: entitlement, extension of self, attention needs, and grandiosity.

An *entitlement attitude* is one where the person feels he has a right to do, say, and receive whatever he wants, by virtue of being who he is. When you think about it, this attitude is similar to that of a toddler who assumes that he is the most important person in the world and should be allowed to do whatever he wishes. Your jealous partner may feel entitled to do any of the following:

- restrict your connections and interactions with others

- demand your undivided attention

- expect you to submit to his orders and the like

- do whatever he wants or tells you to do

The other aspects of an entitlement attitude are the feelings aroused in the person when others do not recognize his desires and don't capitulate. The person can become profoundly hurt, enraged, or shamed. Their subsequent reactions and actions are based on these feelings.

Extension of self refers to psychological boundaries—the extent to which someone has achieved separation and individuation where he understands his self as distinct from others. When these demarcations of self from others are not sufficiently established, the person has difficulty understanding that other people are separate from him, not under his control, and independent. As hard as it may be for you to accept, this way of thinking is not conscious, and he is not aware of how his behavior can reflect his assumptions.

Your jealous partner may exhibit some measure of this under-developed narcissism characteristic. Behaviors that suggest this include the actions listed below:

- telling you what to wear, or insisting that you wear particular clothes or engage in certain acts

- staying in constant contact with you

- not consulting you on family decisions

- volunteering your services without first asking you

- searching your belongings, space, and so on

- not being courteous, such as saying, "Thank you"

- expecting you to have the same opinions, feelings, and ideas as he does

If you have protested to no avail about any acts or attitudes similar to those in the list above, you may want to consider that his extension of self is an underdeveloped part of your partner.

The excessive *need for attention* is very much a part of infants' and children's expectations. They suck up attention like a sponge and come back for more. They have many ways of getting this attention, and not all of them are charming. Now, consider the adult who also has an excessive need for attention but is unaware of this. This adult can go to extremes to keep attention focused on him and gets very uneasy when he is not in the spotlight.

This strong need for attention is a reflection of a deep and enduring yearning for reassurance that he is valued, worthy, and cared for. In some sense, it can also represent the need for external validation that he does, in fact, exist. But, whatever the roots and causes, the current behavior can be troubling to others, and to your relationship. Your jealous partner who has a need for attention can become upset when not in the spotlight, when others (including you) get the attention he feels should be his, or when he tries to gain attention. Examples of attention-seeking behavior include the following:

- talking loudly

- interrupting others to present his thoughts

- moving around constantly, especially when someone else has the attention

- buying, wearing, or doing things to gain attention

- frequently boasting and bragging

- often dealing with and talking about personal problems

- playing one-upmanship games

- needing to win or be shown as superior

The person does not realize that he is seeking attention, will deny it if challenged or confronted, and cannot change his behavior to act in less attention-grabbing ways.

Grandiosity is illustrated by behaviors and attitudes that reflect an inner perception of the self as superior, all-knowing, all-powerful, and wiser than anyone else. This inner perception is not realistic, rational, or objective, but it guides the person to act as if it were all of these. Grandiosity does not permit a person to acknowledge that he has faults or flaws, that he can make mistakes, or that he does not have control over everything in his life. Less grandiosity would give the person a more realistic self-perception, but that would mean that he would have to relinquish his fantasy of superiority, and that is unlikely to happen.

Your jealous partner may have some lingering aspect of infantile grandiosity. The infant has a perception that he "causes" his needs to be met, such as when he is hungry and food is given to him. Further, the infant thinks that others only exist to serve him. In the expected course of development, the child gradually becomes aware of his limitations, and that others are separate and distinct from him. However, there are some people who do not fully develop along expected lines and continue to have some grandiose self-perceptions as adults. Such a person can have some or all of the characteristics listed below:

- has contempt for other people he thinks are inferior

- has a conviction that he is superior and should receive attention, admiration, and deference

- gives orders and expects others to promptly obey them

- exhibits an arrogant attitude

- never admits that he is wrong and makes errors

- expects others to meet his spoken and unspoken needs, wishes, and desires

- tries to organize others' lives according to how he thinks they should be

- tells others what to think, do, feel, wear, and so on

- believes that he should receive preferential treatment

- boasts and brags about himself at every opportunity

Another way that grandiosity occurs is in the person with a hidden or masked inadequate self that has grandiosity as an overlay. The person is primarily grandiose and does not acknowledge or accept that he is anything but all-powerful. The inadequate self can break through at times but is so shameful that the person tries to keep it hidden from himself and from others. When a failure or omission causes the person to feel guilt or shame (grandiosity with an overlay), he may act in the following ways:

- believe that he "causes" other people's feelings

- feel that other capable adults need him in order for them to survive

- consider it his responsibility to maintain harmony at all costs

- feel that other people's needs are more important than his are

- believe that he should be able to prevent an event that is not under his control

- not recognize his limitations and criticize himself for not being more powerful or for not controlling what happens to him or to others

Your jealous partner can exhibit both grandiosity and an impoverished self when he deeply believes that he should be able to "cause" you to act in a certain way. At the same time, he may hide from himself that he fears being too flawed to be lovable and fears that you are poised to leave him at any moment. You may see both parts of him, as they can very quickly switch places. What you may not realize is that he is unaware of both of these states; the switching is not deliberately done to confuse you—it is done to protect the self.

Some self factors that can contribute to jealousy were presented in this chapter, along with a brief description of some aspects of healthy adult narcissism for comparison. You may see your jealous partner's behavior, attitudes, and feelings in some of these self factors but not in others. This is expected, since the descriptions are general and global, not specific and individual. What can be important to remember is that these are emotional states that are deep and enduring, are a result of childhood experiences that continue to affect his behaviors and attitudes, and are hidden and unknown to your partner. Further, these are not caused by you or under your influence or control, nor can you change them or his reactions.

The next chapter presents material that provides information about another factor that can contribute to jealousy: past experiences.

Chapter 4

Past Experiences

The effects of past experiences on your current functioning and relationships can be relatively easy to recognize in many instances (although there are some that are not easy to recognize because they are repressed and denied). However, even forgotten experiences can continue to have a role and impact. These past experiences may play a significant role in your jealous partner's behavior, attitude, and self-perception by feeding the fear of abandonment, confirming a self-perception of not being good enough, and validating her belief that she is not capable of exerting influence and control over herself or the situation.

This discussion focuses on nonfamilial relationships and other experiences throughout life that help to shape perceptions of oneself and feelings and perceptions about others, and it explains how both relate to current feelings, attitudes, and behavior. To begin to understand just how influential these past experiences can be, complete the following exercise.

Exercise 7: Going Back

Materials: Several sheets of paper and a pen or pencil.

Procedure: Find a place to reflect and write that is free from distractions and where you are unlikely to be disturbed.

1. Select a time period in your life: childhood, adolescence, or early adulthood.

2. Close your eyes and try to mentally return to that period, noting feelings, actions, events, people, and relationships that were significant, and anything else that comes to mind. Recall as much detail as possible.

3. When you are ready, open your eyes and write about that period in your life. Begin with something like "This period in my life was . . ."

4. Read what you have written. Make a list of past events, feelings, relationships, and other factors that seem significant or important in some way. These can be positive and pleasurable, or negative and distressing.

5. Read your list and check for any events, feelings, and relationships that are present in your life today. You will probably find two or more that are similar.

There are a number of past experiences that can seem unfinished. Perhaps you did not say good-bye; feelings and reactions important to you were not expressed; you have become aware of someone's impact on you; apologies were not made or appreciation was not expressed; or recalling the person or the events still produces hurt feelings, resentment, or anger in you.

These residual feelings and thoughts about the past can exert conscious and unconscious influences on your current feelings, behavior, and relationships. You cannot go back and change the past, but you can understand its influence on you today, finish some unfinished business, reduce its negative impact on you and your current functioning, and begin to live more fully in the present, thereby reducing the amount of unfinished business you carry to the future.

Your jealous partner is also carrying some unfinished business, as we all do, but hers may be fueling her jealousy, and her perceptions of herself and of you. She is, of course, mainly unaware of this happening, but that does not prevent it from having a negative impact on the relationship.

All past experiences carry some influence on the person, but those experiences that have the most influence can be categorized as either intensely negative or intensely positive. Each individual selects the experiences that carry the most impact for her, usually on an unconscious level. Take a moment to think about this. It is not so much what happens as it is how the person perceives it. What happens may be neutral or positive for someone else, but the same experience may be negative for you, and vice versa. That's why it is so difficult to know which past experiences are continuing to play a major role; they may be on an unconscious level, and they have an individual impact or response.

Even with these difficulties, the discussion can still be helpful. We categorize supportive and satisfying experiences as positive, and experiences involving betrayal, rejection, alienation, and shaming as negative.

Support

Supportive experiences, other than those in your family, helped to form your self-confidence and your self-perception as capable, worthwhile, and valued, and built your self-efficacy. This early support from people in your world helped you to build your own self-acceptance and view others as trustworthy, and it gave you a basis for becoming centered and grounded. You did not have to live with fear of being abandoned or destroyed. Try the following exercise.

Exercise 8: Appreciation and Support

Materials: A sheet of paper and a pen or pencil.

Procedure: Find a place to work where you will not be disturbed. Write a sentence or more about yourself or your experiences with each of the following situations. The sentence should report what did or did not happen for you.

- people, other than family, showing pleasure with me, or something I did
- someone standing up for me and taking my side
- someone expressing appreciation for me as a person
- feeling accepted and valued
- grown-ups saying "please" and "thank you" to me as a child

- someone gently pointing out my mistakes and errors
- feeling that I was an important member of a group
- being asked for my opinion or input
- respect being shown for my decisions
- someone expressing appreciation for my efforts

Read what you have written about yourself and your experiences. Decide whether these statements express a lot of support for you, some support, or very little support. Write your decision at the top of the paper, as you would a title.

Finally, make a list of feelings you have about the support you have received in your life.

You may have some surprises as you complete the exercise. For example, you may realize as you reflect on these that you did receive support from other people but were unaware of it at the time. Or you may realize that you did not get the support you craved or needed. Either way, you now know something about the extent to which you did or did not receive support in your past experiences.

You may want to reflect on how your current behavior and attitudes are still influenced by these past experiences. For example,

- Do you expect to get support from others?

- Are you unsure if you can get support and as a result are a little tentative or even withdrawn?

- Do you assume that others are kindly disposed toward you, or do you assume they are not?

- Do you stay alert for signs of nonsupport or appreciation?

- Are you pleased that others express their support and appreciation of you, or are you disappointed that you receive so little of this?

The kind and amount of support you have received, whether in the present or the past, can affect the quality of your relationships. Likewise, your jealous partner may be reacting in part to her past experiences, especially if they were not supportive of her.

These supportive or nonsupportive experiences continue to play a role in her personal perception about how much others can be trusted, her self-perception about her worth and efficacy, and the extent to which she feels centered and grounded.

Satisfaction

You probably don't have any difficulty seeing that someone who has experienced few, if any, satisfying relationships will be prone to expect that this one—with you—will also fail to be satisfying. These people can stay on edge and feel very threatened by almost everything, since they cannot be confident in their ability to develop and maintain a satisfying relationship.

Let's try to define or describe a satisfying relationship. The following characterize such a relationship:

- Mutual respect and caring are present.

- Partners listen to each other.

- Differences are worked out.

- There is interdependence, and one partner does not dominate or control.

- Individuality and separateness are recognized and accepted.

- Affection and appreciation are expressed.

- Limits of personal responsibility for the other partner's welfare and feelings are recognized.

- Boundaries are respected, and any violations are not intrusive.

- Support for each other is shown.

- Minimal defensiveness is present between the partners.

- Partners enjoy each other.

A satisfying relationship is not automatic; it has to be cultivated. Just think about your most satisfying relationship you had as you were growing up. That relationship probably had all, or most, of the described characteristics. On the other hand, your most unsatisfying relationship likely had few, if any, of these characteristics.

How did this unsatisfying relationship affect you at the time, influence your other relationships, and affect your self-perception and self-confidence? What were some long-term effects on your other relationships? How may this experience be continuing to have an influence on your current behavior, attitudes, and relationships? The effects can be deep, many, and enduring, and they can influence us in unconscious ways.

Just about everyone has had one or more relationships that did not work out, but some people have many such relationships. If asked, some people may not be able to recall having any satisfying relationships. When your relationships have not been satisfying, there is a tendency to be skeptical and leery, and you may even withdraw in new relationships for fear that the new ones will fall apart just like the others.

Partners who have satisfying relationships throughout their lives with family, friends, coworkers, and even acquaintances will most likely not have a deep-seated fear of abandonment and will have confidence in their ability to form and maintain satisfying relationships. They can and do trust others to a reasonable extent and are not always looking for signs of diminishing attention and affection.

There may also be some unfinished business around unsatisfying past relationships for your jealous partner. It is this unfinished business that can influence her jealousy in your relationship. In a sense, what was not finished, closed, or ended in those relationships gets displaced on you and your relationship. Yes, she knows that you are not that person from her past, but something in the current relationship is similar to the past one (it would be rare if there were not any similarities), and it is this similarity that keeps the unfinished business alive, allowing it to influence the relationship with you.

Betrayal

Betrayal and feelings about being betrayed can begin at an early age. If you have ever experienced a brother, sister, cousin, or friend tattling about something you did, then you understand early betrayal. Indeed, children taunt each other by saying, "I'm gonna tell on you." Each little betrayal has an impact, and many such betrayals can accumulate until you have a stack of them, and soon you find it difficult to trust anyone for fear of additional betrayal.

Why do people betray?

- to gain an advantage
- to point out the other person's inadequacies and inferiority
- as confirmation of their superiority
- as revenge for real or imagined acts
- for monetary or other material gain
- to alienate the affection a person is receiving from others in the hope and expectation that it will then be given to them
- to prevent potential harm to themselves
- in response to force or intimidation

The reason for the betrayal is not really important, except when it's done to prevent harm. All other reasons are to give the betrayer something, and that something can be material, such as money; affection, a boost to self-confidence, confirmation of superiority, and so on; and to put the betrayed person at a disadvantage. The real importance of betrayal is the impact on the betrayed person. When you are betrayed you can

- feel like a fool
- become angry or enraged
- experience feelings of shame
- feel inadequate and impotent
- wonder why you were not thought to be good enough by the betrayer
- fantasize or plot revenge

Whatever your reaction, you do not trust that person anymore. There was a relationship between you and the betrayer, there was some trust, and there was a connection to each other, no matter how slight it was. The betrayal showed that the other person did not value the relationship as you did, that she was not worthy of your trust, and that the connection was not meaningful to her. When you are betrayed you are left to deal with the loss of a relationship in addition to realizing that you were inaccurate in your perception of the other person, that your trust was violated, and that there is little or nothing you can do about it. These are not comfortable feelings and, while you can externalize your feelings about being betrayed to the other person, you can still be left with some unconscious negative feelings about yourself. Let's do an exercise that may illustrate this for you.

Exercise 9: Betrayal Feelings

Materials: Paper for drawing, a set of crayons or felt markers, a sheet of paper, and a pen or pencil.

Procedure: Sit in silence in a place where you can work and not be disturbed.

1. Recall an event where you felt betrayed. You may have been a child, teen, or adult. The betrayal may have had significant consequences for you or none at all. That does not matter. Just let the event come to mind, and notice as much as you can about it.

2. When you are ready, use your crayons or markers to draw a picture that illustrates your feelings at that time. The picture can be representative, such as a scene, or abstract, such as splotches of colors.

3. Use the paper and pen or pencil to record all the feelings in the picture, and the feelings you experienced as you thought about the event and drew the picture.

4. Review all you've completed, and let yourself be aware of the continuing impact of that event on you, no matter how mild that impact may be.

This exercise can help you better understand the lingering effects of betrayal, which can increase your sensitivity to the lingering aspects that are probably affecting your jealous partner. She may think that she was not affected, or that she is over a past betrayal, but the feelings do stick around and exert their influence in hidden ways. Exercise 12, at the end of this chapter, may help you bring closure to some of your past experiences and reduce the lingering effects connected to them.

Rejection

Rejection means a lack of connection to the person by that person's choice; it is not your decision, nor is it a mutual one. The fear of abandonment is activated when you feel even the slightest hint of rejection. To be rejected triggers feelings of inadequacy, not being good enough, shame for being fatally flawed, inferiority, worthlessness, helplessness, and hopelessness. The feelings can be faint and fleeting, or intense and enduring. To make these feelings more recognizable, try the following exercise.

Exercise 10: Rejection

Materials: A sheet of paper and a pen or pencil.

Procedure: Sit in a quiet place where you can work and not be disturbed.

1. Reflect on each of the scenarios in step 2, below, and try to put yourself in each position. You may have actually experienced one or more of these; if so, you can use your real experience to help you complete the exercise.

2. Write each of the following down one side of the paper, leaving five or more blank lines between them.

   a. not making the team

   b. not being selected to make a presentation

   c. not being invited to a party

   d. not having a date for a big event

   e. not being asked to join a club

3. Take each of these, one at a time, close your eyes, and think about the feelings that are aroused around the event.

4. When you have the event and feelings set in your mind, open your eyes and, on the blank lines you left under the item, list the thoughts and feelings you had as you did this part of the exercise. Do this for all the listed events.

5. After completing step 4 for all the events, go back over your list of feelings and check or underline all that are thoughts and feelings about yourself. For example, feelings about yourself are embedded in "Why don't they like me?"

6. Make a new list of these thoughts and feelings about yourself. Look at each feeling and decide if it affects a thought about yourself as inferior, inadequate, not valued, helpless, not good enough, shamed, or worthless, and write that description beside the thought or feelings. Read both lists.

This short exercise gives you an increased awareness of the thoughts and ideas that rejection can bring. Some may be mild, such as embarrassment, but some can be intense, such as feeling fatally flawed with no hope of fixing what is flawed.

Almost everyone becomes adept at hiding their real feelings when they are rejected, and some are so adept at hiding that they are able to hide those feelings from themselves. Almost everyone externalizes the rejection to some extent, by faulting the other person for failing to see your value and worth, and by thinking that they are not good enough in some way. That would not be an unusual response, and some anger and resentment could accompany these thoughts. But however much you may be able to externalize your thoughts and feelings about a rejection, you are also having some internal thoughts and feelings about yourself. These internal thoughts and feelings are those that get carried with you as unfinished business from past experiences.

These are also the thoughts and feelings that get activated in your jealous partner. Her past experiences included some rejection, or what felt like rejection. There are circumstances where rejection of the person was not the intent, but the result was that the person did feel rejected. Family events and circumstances, such as divorce and abandonment, could be examples. Insensitivity on the part of family members, friends, teachers, coaches, and other influential adults could also be an example. The person herself having unrealistic expectations of her ability or talent and then being disappointed in herself is another example. However, the thoughts and feelings about herself remain, and so does the fear of abandonment.

Alienation

The jealous partner could feel alienated, or have felt so in the past. Like betrayal and rejection, this is an internal personal state or issue and is not under your control. The person herself generates and controls this feeling. Further, there may be very little in the present that is similar to her past experiences, but this does not prevent these feelings from being activated.

An alienated person feels disconnected from others and either refuses overtures that lead to reconnecting or is unable to reach out and connect. Since humans thrive on having meaningful connections, this inability or failure leads to a sense of being separate or different in a not-so-good way; a strong feeling of loss and grief; and feelings of hurt, rage, resentment, and envy.

Some people seek ways to be unique and special. They want to stand out from the crowd, and they want to get attention and admiration for their differentness. Some may even go to extremes in their search for uniqueness. This behavior seems similar to that of the alienated person, but it is not. Alienation is a lack of an emotional connection to other people—the feeling that you are not an accepted part of a group, and that you are alone in an unfriendly universe. If you have never felt this cut off from other people, you will have difficulty understanding how anyone can feel that way.

People who are alienated typically have experienced considerable rejection; they feel that they have not been valued, prized, or cherished and that they have been treated unfairly. As a result, they tend to be mistrustful of others and keep other people at a distance. They fear being hurt if they should try to connect with other people, and if anyone tries to connect with them, they may assume that the person is being insincere. Some people carry deep and enduring grudges against those they perceive as having rejected or harmed them. They deeply yearn for close connections with other people, and they may envy the positive relationships other people seem to have.

As you can see, there are strong negative feelings related to feeling alienated, and these feelings can push others away just when a person needs the connections the most.

Now, you may never have felt alienated, but many people have experienced this at some point in their lives. If or when you felt alienated, it may have been for a short period when it seemed that nothing was going right in your life, or it may have lasted for some time. But somehow you were able to reestablish meaningful connections to others. What you may not be aware of is that you still carry some of the feelings from that period, especially a fear of abandonment. That fear is a root cause of jealousy; it is the fear that a valued and cherished connection will be severed.

Your jealous partner may also have experienced one or more periods of feeling alienated, and the lasting effects continue to have some impact on her behavior, feelings, and attitude. She doesn't want to experience alienation again, with all of its uncomfortable feelings, and she finds herself compelled to try to keep that from happening—hence her jealous behavior. The fear and dread of abandonment can be easily triggered and they are not understood or controlled by that person. You may not understand either, as her jealous behavior seems not to have a realistic basis and you are not in the process of abandoning her. If neither of you is aware of the lasting effects of previously experienced alienation, the thought that the previous alienation could be affecting your relationship never crosses your mind. You would both continue to react to each other on the basis of known facts and feelings and never touch on this real cause for at least part of the jealousy.

Shame

Milder forms of shame include feelings of embarrassment, unworthiness, and disgracefulness. Almost everyone has experienced some form of shame. Shaming experiences are those that you think reveal your essential self as flawed and unacceptable. These experiences and the feeling of shame they engender are kept hidden from others for fear that, if they became known to others, you would be considered unacceptable and rejected. The felt flaw seems so bad that the person cannot accept this part of her self and keeps it hidden from her self and from others.

Everyone wants to be adequate, capable, lovable, and effective, and to have some power and control. Your self-confidence, self-esteem, and self-efficacy are all dependent on your perceptions of yourself as having these qualities, and the perceptions of others about your qualities. The extent to which these qualities are developed determines the level of confidence, esteem, and efficacy you see in yourself. Every shaming experience can erode these aspects of the self.

The hidden nature of shame can make it difficult to detect and understand shame in ourselves, let alone in anyone else. For example, shame can be the factor fueling someone's anger or rage. She becomes angry to keep from being aware of her shame, or to keep another person from detecting her feeling of shame about her flaws that can never be fixed, her inadequacies, or her belief that she is not good enough or that her self is unlovable and unacceptable.

To keep these very painful awarenesses out of her consciousness, the person can externalize them, declaring others to be extremely flawed and unworthy and projecting the feelings of shame onto another person, and act toward that person as if they had the unwanted and unacceptable parts of her self. Or she can internalize them and use her defenses to keep them out of her awareness. Let's try an example to illustrate these possibilities.

> Larry is jealous toward Sharon, and his jealousy is roused when she laughs and talks with their child's softball coach. Larry's feeling in the moment is anger, but that anger is masking an unconscious self-perception that he is not good enough (shame). He would probably deny it if anyone were to suggest he felt that way about himself.
>
> If Larry externalized his anger and projected it on Sharon, he might do something like ask her what her problem is, respond to the anger he's projected onto Sharon with additional anger, and become even more enraged because he now sees Sharon as angry at him.
>
> If Larry were to internalize the anger and shame, he would suppress his emotions. He would simply ignore his anger and shame around the incident, but they would smolder in his nonconscious ready to spring to life in a moment.

This is a very simplified example, but I think it conveys the basic idea. Anger, hurt, resentment, and similar emotions can mask hidden feelings of shame about oneself. Try the following exercise to get a notion of how your shame may be masked.

Exercise 11: *Masking Shame*

Materials: Two or more sheets of paper and a pen or pencil.

Procedure: Find a place to work where you will not be disturbed. Read each item and respond to it before moving to the next one.

1. Think about a time when you were at a gathering of people you knew, such as a meeting, bar, party, or church function. Now, imagine that, after the event has been going on for a while, someone new joins the group.

2. Take each of the following characteristics or attributes separately, and visualize the new person as having it. Write down the feelings you experience as you see the new person, with the designated characteristic, joining the group.

The new person is

   a. dressed better and more expensively than you are

   b. has attained a higher status or greater achievements than you have

   c. receives admiring glances from others in the group

   d. gets compliments

   e. is obviously wealthier than you are

   f. is younger, taller, slimmer, and more attractive than you are

3. Look at your list of feelings. Note how many are direct expressions of your shame (e.g., feelings of inadequacy or awkwardness), and how many are indirect and masked (e.g., feelings of intimidation, resentment, or rejection).

4. On another sheet of paper, write a sentence about how you generally respond or act when you have these feelings. For example, you might write, "When I feel inadequate, I withdraw from interactions," or "When I feel inadequate, I find fault with the person whose presence generated that feeling."

Your jealous partner may have experienced many events in her life where her shame was triggered and so has developed better masking capabilities. She now experiences shame with a masking overlay of another feeling, such as anger; the overlay is the one that is expressed, and the one that you see. Understanding that shame underlies some of your partner's jealousy and its expressions can help you cope better by learning to not react, or overreact, to the overlay feeling, but to be more understanding of the underlying shame.

Reducing the Impact of Your Past Experiences

The preceding discussion described how some past experiences can play a role in the irrational jealousy your partner exhibits. Some experiences remain as unfinished business on the conscious and unconscious levels, and they exert influences in direct and indirect ways until closure is attained. These experiences are finished or closed when one can remember them without a great deal of emotion being aroused. These feelings are not suppressed, repressed, or denied—they are truly gone or well integrated. The memory is still intact, and you can recall how you felt at that time, but the feelings are recognized as being in the past. Achieving closure can be more easily accomplished for experiences that you carry on the conscious level, and it takes considerable personal work with a competent therapist to do this for what remains on the unconscious level.

Memories of some of your past experiences and their associated feelings may have been aroused in you as you read this chapter. The following exercise is one possible way to let go of some of the distressing feelings.

Exercise 12: Letting Go of Those Feelings

Materials: Colored paper, a pen or pencil, and four small boxes.

Procedure: Find a place to work where you will not be disturbed.

1. Cut 8 to 10 strips of each of the following paper colors as noted, for different past experiences: red strips for betrayal, green strips for rejection, purple strips for alienation, and orange strips for shame.

2. Put the strips in color-coded piles. Start with the red strips. Write all the feelings aroused in you as you thought of your past betrayal experiences on these strips, one feeling to a strip. Do the same for the other colors and experiences.

3. Put each set of strips in a different box, and place the boxes on a table or on the floor in a row where you can see them.

4. Look at the boxes and recall some of the feelings each contains. Then, close your eyes, and visualize the strips dissolving, burning, flying away, or otherwise leaving in some form.

5. Open your eyes, pick up the boxes, and dispose of them. You can put them in the recycling bin or garbage can, burn them, or whatever. Pay particular attention to how you feel when you dispose of the boxes, and say to yourself, "I can let go of these feelings." Note how you feel as you do this, and note which feelings you have difficulty releasing.

Chapter 5

Family of Origin Experiences

Your experiences in your family of origin have helped shape you throughout your life. They have had a lasting and significant influence on the person you are today. Although there are many other influences and experiences that have helped make you who you are, the family ones are the deepest. As a result they can also be the least accessible ones, because so many significant experiences occurred when you were in the preverbal level of development, that is, when you were an infant and child. The same is true for your jealous partner, even though his experiences were different from yours.

What family of origin experiences could play a role in your partner's jealousy? It's not possible to describe all the experiences that could have a role, nor is it possible to know the specific ones for your partner. You have to read the ones presented in this chapter as hypotheses that may never be tested or examined, and as possibilities that can never be verified by you. What is presented here is intended to increase your awareness of your family of origin experiences and help you better understand how your partner's experiences could be a part of her jealousy. Further, only a small set of such experiences is presented here.

The examples and categories of family of origin experiences that are addressed in this chapter are mirroring and empathy, parental destructive narcissism, sibling rivalry, parental rivalry, parental perceptions, abandonment issues, and destruction issues.

Mirroring and Empathy

Babies think they are wonderful, and they respond beautifully to everyone who mirrors their self-perception. The more mirroring they get, the more it builds their sense of self as adequate, valued, and worthwhile. This seems to also be true of empathy: the more the baby gets his needs met and his caregiver seems to understand his feelings of discomfort or pleasure, the more it contributes to a strong sense of self.

You may have noticed that babies constantly look at their mother's (or caregiver's) face, and that some babies can get very upset when they cannot see their mother's face. It is this face that provides the mirroring of the baby's feelings and internal state. For example, when a baby feels uncomfortable, his mother's face can reflect the discomfort because the mother is empathizing with that discomfort (while acting to reduce or eliminate that discomfort, such as by feeding or changing a diaper). The same process takes place with regard to the baby's delight with himself, when the mother affirms and reflects that perception with smiles and words about how wonderful the baby is.

Fast-forward for just a moment through your childhood, adolescence, and adulthood. Think of the people with whom you became intimate, for example, friends, lovers, and spouse; try to recall their facial expressions when they looked at you during the relationship, especially at the beginning. Their faces probably mirrored your delight at the more positive aspects of your self, and you responded to this mirroring by being attracted to that person. Even if you generally tend to focus on the more negative aspects of yourself, you respond positively to those who can see your positive aspects.

The above is an example of how family of origin experiences continue to exert influence during the course of life. However, mothers are not the only ones to provide mirroring and empathy, since there are other people in a baby's world. These people also provide some reflection of the baby's self-perception, hopefully positive. All these mirroring and empathy experiences are stored in a baby's mind to help form and shape his self-confidence, self-esteem, and self-efficacy.

What can happen when a baby does not experience mirroring and empathy? It was hypothesized by D. W. Winnicott (1960) that the baby finds that his "real self" is not mirrored, and so a "false self" emerges that is more to the mother's (or caregiver's) liking, and the false self gets reinforced. The false self then becomes the self presented to the world, and the person hides his true self.

As the person grows and develops, he continues to keep the real self under wraps so that others will not see it, is ashamed and afraid of the true self, and resists all efforts by the true self to emerge. This plays out in the following behaviors and attitudes, for example:

- being nice all of the time

- never experiencing or expressing uncomfortable feelings

- accepting unwarranted responsibility for others' feelings

- taking the responsibility to maintain harmony

- giving in to others' wants, needs, and wishes

- failing to develop a personal identity separate and distinct from others

- being easily offended

- being hypersensitive to perceived criticism or disapproval

It takes a lot of effort to keep the real self hidden and repressed, and that effort can siphon off energy that could be spent in more constructive ways, such as self-reflection and building honest relationships.

Try the following exercise to see if you reflect your partner's positive or negative self-perception.

Exercise 13: *Mirroring*

Materials: A sheet of paper and a pen or pencil.

Procedure: Sit in silence in a place where you will not be disturbed and close your eyes.

1. Recall a situation where your partner was jealous. Let the scene play out, remembering as many of your feelings and words as you can.

2. When you are ready, open your eyes and make a list of the feeling words, phrases, and thoughts about your partner that you expressed or experienced during the event.

3. Examine your list and check all the words and feelings that are positive.

4. Close your eyes again to recall the scene. This time, really look at your partner and what you recall of his facial expressions. See if any of your words or feelings could also be reflective of his self-perception. That is, if you were feeling inadequate, could you also be reflecting his self-perception of inadequacy? Check all the negative words, feelings, and thoughts.

It would be unusual if you did not find that you were mirroring any of his self-perceptions. By doing the exercise, you have made yourself more aware that you may often be mirroring your partner's feelings and thoughts about himself.

At certain times, like the one you reflected on in the exercise, you may be open to "catching" your partner's feelings. Yes, you are experiencing your own feelings, but you may also be catching some of his and making them your feelings. The stronger and more resilient your psychological boundaries are, and the more centered and grounded you are, the less you will catch his feelings.

Parental Destructive Narcissism

This topic is the focus and theme of my book *Children of the Self-Absorbed* (Brown 2001). Children of a parent or parents with a destructive narcissistic pattern were expected to always please the parent and were not allowed to develop a separate and distinct identity apart from the parent. The effects of such an upbringing are significant, deep, and enduring. The child does not realize what is happening and can fail to develop psychologically in very important ways.

Having a self-absorbed parent can produce an adult who is constantly on edge and alert for cues from others. If your partner is the child of a self-absorbed parent, this could translate to your partner's constant attention to you and whatever you are doing as a means to try to stay in touch with your feelings and needs. Thus, when he sees you responding positively to someone else, he can assume that the person is meeting your needs. This can produce feelings in him that he is inadequate and has failed to meet your needs, just as his destructive narcissistic parent(s) gave him the responsibility of meeting their emotional needs and shamed him when he failed to do so. This expectation to meet others' needs and the resulting feelings are so ingrained in him that he does not know they are there, but acts on them in unconscious ways.

What is parental destructive narcissism? This occurs when a parent is so self-absorbed that, instead of the parent caring for the psychological and emotional well-being of the child, the reverse takes place. That is, the child is expected to take care of the parent's well-being. The child is not loved and cared for as a separate person—the child gets these only when he is able to please the parent. Thus, from birth on, the child is seeking to please the parent. This state can produce an adult who is very insecure and derives his sense of being worthy and valued from paying constant attention to the cues from others. He doesn't have the security and confidence of being valued and loved as a worthwhile individual, as some people do when they receive adequate mirroring and empathy from the parent(s), as described in the previous section.

Destructive Narcissism Characteristics

Below is a list of some characteristics that, when they appear in a cluster, may be seen in a person with a destructive narcisstic pattern:

- perceives others as extensions of self and thus, under his control
- wants to be thought of as unique and special
- lacks recognition that you are a separate individual
- expects you to meet his emotional needs
- engages in admiration-seeking behavior
- blames, shames you for failure to meet his needs; lacks empathy
- grandiosity
- expects you to read his mind and take care of him
- does not recognize or respect boundaries
- has an entitlement attitude

The child who grows up under these parental conditions may, as an adult, have some characteristics of a destructive narcissistic pattern (DNP) or some of the more troubling attitudes and behaviors reflective of the failure to develop his self according to expected stages. For example, he may not have completed separation and individuation sufficiently to fully understand that he is a distinct individual. Thus, he does not respect others' boundaries, considers others to be an extension of him and under his control, and constantly seeks attention and admiration. If his response to being "parentified" was a compliant one, he can behave like the clinging jealous partner discussed in chapter 7. If his response was a rebellious one, he may behave as the reactive or manipulative jealous partners discussed in chapters 7 and 8. Whatever the outcome, a child reared by one or more parents with a DNP will experience some lasting effects.

Sibling Rivalry

The birth of a sibling can be very traumatic for some children, and they may never fully recover from being supplanted by the newcomer. Careful preparation for the arrival by the parents can do much to assist the child to accept his sibling, but even the most thoughtful and sensitive preparation is limited in this respect. Children are often excited about the prospect of gaining a sister or brother, but the reality stirs up jealousy, resentment, and fear. The parent who has tried to prepare the child may hear him say things like the following after the sibling is born:

"Put her back in your stomach."

"I wish he wasn't here."

"Give her away."

"Make him go away."

"I don't want her for my sister."

"Why did you have to have him?"

Now, if a well-prepared child says thing like this, just think of what a child might do and say if he is not well prepared, or not at all prepared. He will express his feelings in some way, and not necessarily the most acceptable ways.

Regardless of the extent to which a child is prepared for the birth or adoption of a sibling, there are still changes in the child's world that he cannot understand, simply because he is a child and does not yet have the capacity for understanding himself, his environment, and the impact of these changes. Unable to fully understand what these changes mean, he observes that his parents give the newcomer time, attention, and care, and that he gets less of these than he did before the baby arrived.

That's just a small part of what can happen at the introduction of a sibling. There are many other events and family circumstances that can exacerbate sibling rivalry, which can continue throughout the person's life. If the old feelings are not resolved, the jealousy and fear around the arrival of the sibling stand ready to emerge at any time. These feelings then get replayed and reemerge whenever that person thinks that the affection, time, and attention that are his are in danger of being given, or seduced, away to someone else. The threat becomes that of both the earlier perceived loss and the potential for a current loss.

It can be important to remember that a child can feel both love and resentment for the sibling. The person is conflicted. He wants to get rid of the sibling, but he also wants to keep the sibling. Many times these feelings are not understood or integrated, and they remain as polarities, two opposite feelings, within that person. The younger the child was when the sibling was born or introduced into the family, the less likely these jealous feelings were worked through, understood, and integrated.

Your understanding of the deep-seated and enduring feelings of jealousy, hurt, resentment, and fears that your partner may have, and that are reemerging in your relationship with him, can assist your coping. You must accept that your partner is unaware of this. Telling him will not help the situation at all, and you cannot fix or compensate for the effects that the introduction of the sibling had earlier in life. Your understanding can help you maintain your equanimity, reduce your negative feelings about your partner and yourself, and respond appropriately without lashing out.

Parental Rivalry

Some parents have such deep-seated fears of inadequacy and abandonment, underdeveloped narcissism, or other unresolved issues that they become their own children's rivals. They may compete with their children for attention, admiration, affection, power, and control.

An adult who competes with a child is unable to successfully compete with other adults. He may compete with a child because he needs constant reassurance of his worth and has a big inner deficit that he is unwittingly seeking to overcome or to fill. Just as he is probably unaware of the continuing issues and underdeveloped aspects of himself that need work, he is unable to see the child as a child, only as a competitor. The child who grows up with a parent who competes with him tries or fights harder to keep what he has because he has so often lost in the competition with his parent.

The following four examples of parental rivalry may help to illustrate what is meant here. Try to put yourself in the child's position, and think about what the child might possibly feel under the described circumstances.

> Lew overhears his parents arguing about how much attention his mother gives him. His mother says that she feels she needs to stay home with Lew while his father goes to his office party. His father tells his mother in an angry voice that she is spoiling Lew, and there is no reason why she can't go to the office party with him.

> Rebecca gets a hug and kiss from her father, who tells her how pretty she looks in her new dress. As he does this, her mother enters the room and immediately yells at Rebecca to go back to her room and clean it up. Rebecca's mother glares at the father.

> Sam is chosen to be on the academic challenge team and is very excited about it. At a birthday dinner for his grandmother, he is chatty and outgoing, telling everyone what a great opportunity this will be. His father immediately begins to monopolize the conversation with stories about his sports achievements during his school years.

> A friend of the family tells Mona's father how wonderful it is that Mona has won so many prizes for her musical accomplishments. Her father responds that he taught her from the beginning, and that if it were not for him, she would not have received any prizes.

Parental rivalry can also appear as tearing down the child's confidence. Parents who compete with their child may do the following:

- insist that everything he does must be perfect

- point out and emphasize even small errors or mistakes

- make unfair comparisons with other children

- comment on the child's flaws or inadequacies

- make demeaning comments or put-downs

- fail to recognize what the child does accomplish, or does well

- focus on misbehavior and not acknowledge good or appropriate behavior

The child receives and internalizes the message that he is not good enough in his parent's opinion, and continues to act on that internalized message.

Rivalry or competition means that there are winners and there are losers. The rival parent has more resources and experiences at his disposal and will generally outdo the child. This sets up another scenario that gets played out in the child's subsequent relationships: the need to compete and the fear of losing. Because the child is usually at a disadvantage in a competition with a parent, when he becomes an adult, he does not recognize when he has won and continues to feel he has lost, no matter how favorable to him the outcome was. He may stay in the defensive or attacking state even when the competition is over. This can be really confusing for you, since you don't know or understand why he cannot let go.

Parental rivalry can be subtle, masked, or minimized, but it still has lasting effects on the child. The parent is probably not aware of his tendency to compete with the child and, if challenged or confronted, would shrug it off as a way of teaching the child about the "real" world. What is most likely happening is that this parent is more concerned about meeting his personal needs and lacks empathy for the child as he suffers from the effects of this competitive behavior.

Parental Perceptions

Take a moment to complete the following exercise.

Exercise 14: *Parental Perceptions of Me*

Materials: Two or more sheets of paper and a pen or pencil.

Procedure: Find a place to work where you will not be disturbed.

1. Close your eyes and bring up an image of your mother's face looking at you when you were a child, during the early teen years, and during the late teen years. What messages did you receive regarding her perceptions and feelings about you for the following?

   - your physical appearance

   - your lovability

   - your intellectual ability

   - your talents or other abilities, such as in sports

   - your effectiveness

2. When you are ready, open your eyes and write a list of the messages, positive and negative, you received from your mother.

3. Now, do the same for your father. Then repeat for the other important adults in your life, such as a stepparent or grandparent.

4. Review your lists. Note similarities and differences between these messages. Think about the messages you may have unconsciously internalized and may be acting on without realizing it.

5. Note how many of the messages were positive and how many were negative. If you are lucky, you will have more positive messages than negative ones. Unfortunately, many people receive more negative messages, and your partner may be one of those people.

When you get negative messages about your parents' perceptions of you, these are internalized, and they have the potential to become core beliefs about yourself. In adulthood, these old messages can be triggered at any time, and they can have a signifi-cant effect on your attitudes and behavior. They are difficult to root out and change. Part of the process of becoming an adult with strong and resilient boundaries and a strong self-identity is to gain an understanding of these old parental messages and adopt your own messages about yourself. The process requires some self-reflection and self-examination—about who you are and the person you want to be. You may find that you want to retain some parental messages because they seem to fit you, adapt other messages, and discard some. When you decide to keep or adapt these messages, you will make them yours; and you will no longer act on them because of unconscious internalization and identifica-tion. They will be freely chosen.

Your partner may be aware of some of his parental percep-tions of him, but he is most likely unaware of many more. Because you are an observer, you cannot know what perceptions he is aware of. However much he is conscious of his parental perceptions, he is still identifying with some of these old messages, and these are con-tributing to some of his behaviors and attitudes. You don't know, he doesn't know, and some of this cannot be known except through considerable personal work on his part. These messages can have a powerful influence on your partner's self-confidence, self-esteem, and self-efficacy, and all of these in turn contribute to his jealousy.

Let's do a final exercise about parental perceptions.

Exercise 15: An Introduction

Materials: A sheet of paper and a pen or pencil.

Procedure: Find a place to work where you will not be disturbed.

1. Put yourself in the following scene:

   Your mother (or father) has to introduce you to a very important person. This person is interested in your char-acter, temperament, personal characteristics, and abili-ties. Write what you think your parent would say in his or her introduction of you. Write as much as you wish.

2. Review what you have written, and check the positive comments. Ask yourself if these ring true according to how you perceive yourself.

3. Review what you have written and check the negative comments. Ask yourself if these ring true according to how you perceive yourself.

4. Review any comments that were not checked. How true do these seem when compared to your self-perception?

5. Reviewing the comments, look for any parental messages you have internalized, and those you identify with. Note which ones you will now freely choose as part of your self-perception, and which ones you can let go. (If someone else perceives these as a characteristic, that's their perception. It is not your self-perception.)

Abandonment Issues

Safety is a basic human need. Feeling insecure and unsafe can cause the fight-or-flight defense. The person who feels anxious can mobilize his resources to combat the perceived danger and make himself feel safe. Everyone responds this way when threatened. The difference among individuals lies in what is perceived as threatening, anxiety producing, and dangerous.

Individual perceptions and reactions to psychological threats to one's safety are formed from life experiences beginning at birth. The infant or child who is neglected or abused, handled impersonally, not responded to empathically, "parentified," or part of a chaotic family can develop fears of abandonment that stay with him throughout his life. These become a basic part of who he is, exerting their influences on his self-perceptions and reactions on an unconscious level.

To understand fear of abandonment, try the following exercise.

Exercise 16: Feeling Abandoned

Materials: Several sheets of paper a pen or pencil, and a set of crayons or felt-tip markers.

Procedure: Find a place to work where you will not be disturbed.

1. Recall an incident or event like any of the following:

   - You are not invited to a party.
   - Friends have gone off and left you.
   - You find out that you were not told about an important event that had happened to a family member or friend.
   - You move to a new place where you do not know anyone.
   - You come home at your regular time and unexpectedly find no one there.
   - You feel left out or alienated.
   - You don't have anyone to sit with at lunchtime.
   - No one asks you to join in at a party, dance, or other social event.
   - A parent leaves home for an extended period of time.
   - Someone close to you dies.

2. Draw a picture that illustrates the event.

3. On another sheet of paper, write a paragraph or more about that experience. List all the feelings you remember having then, and all the feelings you have now as you work through this event.

4. Give the intensity of the feelings you felt at that time a rating of 0 to 10, where 0 is little or no intensity and 10 is extremely high intensity. If you cried, became angry, or otherwise outwardly expressed your feelings, the intensity should be rated 6 or higher.

5. Review all you have done: drawing, writing, listing, and rating. Note any lingering feelings you are having as you do this exercise.

It is probably safe to say that everyone has felt some level of abandonment at some point in his life. However, each person reacts differently, and this difference is based on the person's individual characteristics, which interact with his early life experiences (i.e., how he was nurtured and cared for) and subsequent events in his life (especially those over which he had no control, such as a parent's leaving or death). These set the stage for how and when the fear of abandonment will get triggered.

Your jealous partner is in the grips of his fear combined with his other characteristics and feelings. His fear that you are emotionally and psychologically abandoning him can arouse dread, panic, fury, and the like. Because he is unlikely to understand why he feels the way he does, his efforts to control, reduce, or eliminate his jealousy do not succeed. His jealousy is deep and enduring, and some of the events that helped to establish it are buried in his preverbal memory.

Fear of Destruction

This fear encompasses real and external, fantasized, and psychological dangers to the self. Real dangers do exist, but they are not always identifiable, such as substance abuse or a partner's potential for physical abuse. There are also numerous fantasized dangers; children especially can have many of these, such as when they imagine monsters under their bed. Psychological dangers are specific for each person, but all involve some level or degree of the following:

- The self is not strong enough to prevent being shattered.

- Boundaries are not adequate to prevent being taken over.

- The self is incomplete.

- The self is fragmented.

Whenever the self is in danger of no longer existing, and to prevent this from happening, the person will go to extreme measures.

Both external and internal assaults can pose psychological danger. Basically, all psychological assaults are internal, since it is that individual's perception of the danger and of his adequacy to face it that determines if and how the assault will receive a response. External assaults are those that other people, events, and circumstances launch, which lead to the internal assault. For example, you may think that you are adequate, good enough, and the like. However, imagine that you start to feel insecure and intimidated when you have to interact with the CEO of your company, who is very forceful, domineering, and abrupt. The initial assault comes from the outside, that is, the CEO who uses his position and status in a powerful and insensitive way, but your internal responses to the CEO are your personal perceptions that your self is in danger when you start to feel insecure and intimidated. Suppose you do not feel insecure and intimidated in your interactions with this same CEO. This would produce a very different response on your part.

Your jealous partner may go through a similar sequence when he encounters a threatening person, event, or circumstance. His fear of destruction emerges: he does not feel that he has the resources to repel the external assault and feels that his internal resources are not sufficient to prevent an internal assault. He sees himself as being in an extremely dangerous position and fights to preserve his self from destruction. He also defends himself from having an awareness of his internal state by using defenses like some of the following:

- *rationalization:* using external reasons to explain or excuse his behavior

- *deflection:* blaming others

- *displacement:* becoming angry at an inanimate object or someone else

- *withdrawal:* sulking, pouting, or giving the silent treatment

- *denial:* substance abuse, overeating, gambling, or excessive shopping

Some jealous partners will act on the premise that the best defense is a good offense. They may act out their anger and distress in ways that are intended to hurt the other person. These ways can be psychological and relational, or physical. Physical expressions of anger are never acceptable, and the recipient of these behaviors should seek a way out of the relationship. Violence, rape, and other physical forms of subjugation are all illegal; there are organizations and laws designed to help anyone in that sort of situation.

Psychologically offensive behaviors can include some of the following:

- sarcasm, cutting remarks, and the like

- retaliatory acts to incur your jealousy

- starting a fight with you about something else

- finding fault with you about almost everything

- making demeaning and devaluing remarks about you

- determining your sensitive areas, and focusing on them

The recipient of these behaviors can become demoralized, depressed, or prone to retaliate in some way. Retaliation just makes a bad situation worse, and your becoming demoralized or depressed does not help you, your partner, or the relationship. It seems as if your jealous partner, who fears the destruction of his self, sets out to make sure that he is indeed destroyed. The decline or loss of the relationship affects his self-perception of adequacy, efficacy, and worthiness.

This chapter focused on family of origin factors that can contribute to jealousy. As you have learned, family experiences, combined with personal characteristics, life experiences with people other than relatives, and the person's perceptions of some immediate factors, can lead to an individual, distinct form of jealousy in each person. The intent of this presentation was to help you become aware of just how complex your partner's jealousy is, how much is hidden from him and from you, why it can be difficult for him to change his jealous behavior and feelings, and why you cannot effect change for him.

Chapter 6

The Jealous Partner: Clingy and Reactive Styles

Chapters 6 and 7 discuss four general jealousy styles; clingy, reactive (paranoid), manipulative, and exhibitionistic. Each person is different and has her own unique style of jealous behaviors and attitudes. However, you may better understand your jealous partner's style after reading these chapters, and that information, along with some understanding of the factors that fuel your partner's jealousy, can lead you to finding or creating ways to better cope with it.

The Clingy Style

We begin by examining your partner's behaviors and attitudes that categorize the clingy style. Rate the extent to which you think your partner does, thinks, or feels each of the following using the designated scale. Most of the items require your inference, since the feelings and thoughts may not be directly observed. We are more interested in your perceptions than in the correctness of your judgments.

Scale 1: The Clinging Jealous Partner Scale	
Use the following scale to rate your partner's clingy behaviors, attitudes, and feelings. 5—always, or almost always 4—frequently 3—sometimes 2—seldom 1—never, or almost never	
1. Your partner becomes anxious when you are not with her.	
2. Your partner is alert to signs of your distress, intentions, attention, or affection.	
3. Your partner asks for reassurance that you care for her or that she is needed.	
4. Your partner smothers you with affection and attention.	
5. Your partner tries to read your mind and anticipate what you want or need.	
6. Your partner seems to be desperately trying to "get it right."	
7. Your partner may subjugate her needs in favor of yours.	
8. Your partner seems to be seeking fusion or enmeshment with you.	
9. Your partner is hypersensitive to perceived criticism.	
10. Your partner is easily hurt emotionally.	

Scoring

Add your ratings to derive a total score. A rating of 41 to 50 indicates a severe clingy style; 31 to 40 indicates a strong clingy style; 21 to 30 indicates a moderate clingy style; 11 to 20 indicates a tendency to be clingy at times; and a 0 to 10 indicates little or no tendency to be clingy. A brief explanation of each item is presented below. If you gave your partner a rating of 20 or more, pay particular attention to the descriptions.

Anxiety

Your jealous partner may become anxious when she cannot see you, like the infant who assumes that when she does not see her caregiver, for example, that the person has disappeared and will not return. The child becomes very upset and cries until the person reappears. Or the anxiousness can be like that of a parent who fears for the safety of her child when the parent is not on hand to protect her from real or fantasized danger, or like that of a parent who worries that the child will get into mischief whenever she is not around. Regardless, your absence produces some anxiety for her.

At the beginning of your relationship, you may have liked that she wanted you near her all the time, and so you tried to give her what she wanted. You may have felt some slight irritation at times, but overall you did not object to her wanting you around. You probably also had some nonconscious expectation that she would become less anxious over time after she realized that you did care for her and would always return. However, that shift did not occur. She remained anxious, and this anxiousness has revealed itself in many ways, such as the following:

- phoning you frequently just to check in or chat

- expecting you to arrive at a regular time, and becoming upset when you are late

- interrupting your workday with a call or visit

- expecting you to notify her if you intended to be ten to fifteen minutes late

- wanting you to recount every detail of what you do and think about when you are away from her

- asking constant questions about what you do or think when you are not with her

- attempting to make you feel guilty and insensitive when you don't call or arrive at the expected time

Your partner is making you responsible for her anxiousness. You are put in a position where your acts, and failures to act, are deemed the cause of her anxiety, and she takes this as a signal that you don't care for her or would prefer someone else. She doesn't see or accept that she is responsible for her feelings of anxiety, nor does she accept that you can never do enough to relieve her anxiety.

Alertness to Signs of Distress

The clingy jealous partner can stay in a constant state of tension, ever alert for signs of your distress, discomfort, intent, attention, and affection. She is so anxious to please that she is on edge all the time, fearing that she will miss an important signal and fail you in some way. She may even perceive your social inter-actions with strangers, acquaintances, colleagues, and other distant people as indications of her failure to notice what you wanted, or signs that you are more attracted to them.

Some sensitivity to your needs and moods is desirable in a partner, and you probably appreciated this at the beginning of the relationship. As time went on, however, you began to want some space and saw nothing wrong with being cordial, pleasant, and courteous to other people. What seemed to be sensitivity and caring at first soon became cloying and smothering. You may even have been confused by her over-the-top reactions of jealousy.

You may suspect that even if you gave all your attention and affection to your partner it would not be sufficient to satisfy her. You are correct. She can never get enough reassurance that she is worthy of being loved and cared for, is valued as a worthwhile person, is able to survive on her own, is not in danger of being abandoned, would not be destroyed if you should leave, and is capable and effective.

Needing Constant Reassurance

Your partner can never get sufficient reassurance, and she is probably not shy about letting you know when she wants or needs it. You probably know her so well that you are able to pick up on her nonverbal cries for reassurance, or the scene may have been set to keep you in a constant state of providing reassurance.

Beneath her need for reassurance are profound and deep feelings of inadequacy, impending doom, shame for being flawed, guilt for not measuring up to others' expectations, and fear of being abandoned or destroyed. She does not feel capable, competent, lovable, wanted, or valued as she is, and no amount of reassurance can give her these feelings about herself. These are internal states or perceptions that propel her to look to external sources to tell her that she is wrong in her self-perceptions, and every time she does not receive what she seeks, she takes that as validation of her negative self-perceptions.

Providing constant reassurance can get to be tiring and even irritating. You don't understand why your positive reassurances and perceptions of her are not enough. Further, she may have achieved and demonstrated competence in many areas and exhibit confidence on the surface. This can be confusing to you. What may be happening is that she does not believe that she has achieved anything on her own, that she is an imposter who has fooled others, and that she may be exposed at any moment; she exhibits a false self-confidence to hide these self-perceptions. Her constant cries for reassurance carry her hope that she will not be exposed and revealed as incompetent or inadequate. Ironically, she may already be what she wants to be but cannot see it.

Her jealousy can be aroused at any time regardless of what you do, say, or mean. She carries a self-perception that she is not good enough to meet your needs and expectations, and that, because she is this way, you are poised to leave and reject her. You will not be able to convince her otherwise.

Smothering You with Affection

It is difficult to describe smothering affection, as each person has different acceptance levels. Some cannot get too much affection, while others are content with "enough." Thus, whether your partner smothers you is up to you to decide.

Some indices of smothering are your reactions to your partner's displays of affection. Do you ever feel that you are being overwhelmed with her affection and want her to back off some? Do you ever wonder if the display of affection is sincere, or if it is being used to manipulate you in some way? Have you ever been embarrassed at displays of affection by your partner or felt that they were inappropriate for the setting? Does your partner try to get you out of a "mood" by showing affection instead of letting you work your way out of it? Do you ever feel guilty for wishing that she would leave you alone just this once? Do you feel that you cannot possibly return the depth and extent of the affection she shows you? These are some examples of feelings and reactions in response to being smothered. It is hard to reject, push away, or remove yourself from affection, since you do want some, but just not this much. There may be times when you feel you cannot breathe, but you know that if you were to say that, your partner would be hurt. You don't have good choices when you feel you are being smothered.

Mind Reading

Your partner may have some irrational beliefs about herself that keep her in a constant state of tension trying to read your mind and anticipate your wants, needs, and desires. These irrational beliefs were developed at an early age in response to a parental expectation that she should take care of them. She grew up with this internalized message and it is so much a part of her that she is unaware that it exists.

Some behaviors that may indicate your partner's mind-reading tendencies are the following:

- constantly looking at you and noticing your every move

- asking you about your likes and dislikes in minute detail

- being extra sensitive to your moods

- accurately reading your nonverbal communication

- wanting to know if she "got it right" about almost everything

- becoming very anxious or upset when you withdraw, want to have some space and time for yourself, or just don't feel like talking

- wanting to be involved in everything you do

- looking to you for nonverbal cues about her looks, dress, and activities

Many of these behaviors, on a modest level, are part of an intimate relationship. However, the person who grew up being expected to read her parents' minds carries it to an extreme. You may find that you are "catching" her tension and edginess without being aware that you are doing so, and you don't understand why you feel as you do. This "catching" may be part of your desire to detach, withdraw, or flee. Sometimes you have a strong need to do this, and when you act on this need, it seems to make your partner try harder, and so the circular action begins. She tries harder, you become tenser and try to get away in some fashion, she tries even harder, and that just makes you want to get away even more.

Wanting to Get It Right

Striving for perfection may be an admirable pursuit. However, perfection is not always definable and the concept of perfection may differ from person to person. Also, it cannot be attained in many instances, and it can sometimes seem to be a moving target. There is no rational reason to expect yourself to always be perfect. Nevertheless, your partner may have this expectation for herself, and for you. If she believes that she must always be perfect, she can also have the notion that she is wrong, inadequate, and shameful whenever she fails to be perfect. It's not so much that the person wants to be perfect and works to achieve it as it is that she takes on negative and irrational beliefs about herself when she doesn't achieve perfection, which often occurs.

Your clinging partner may be driving both of you up the wall with her need to "get it right." While at first you may have perceived her high standards as praiseworthy, they have become frustrating and annoying. She may even be constantly nagging you about the least little thing you don't do "right," or for not being dedicated to achieving perfection. Neither of these is helpful in a relationship.

Your partner may be reacting to old parental messages about her worth, value, and adequacy that told her of the need and expectation for her to be perfect. This was internalized and has become a part of her core self, and she now feels intensely anxious and shamed when she fails to be perfect or "get it right." She also may think only in terms of right or wrong, good or bad, perfect or imperfect. The concepts of just good enough, adequate, and sufficient are not understood or accepted by her. Ambiguity, gradations, levels, and the like are not understood and produce much anxiety.

This need to "get it right" can extend to your relationship: she feels she is not getting it right when she becomes jealous. That is, she thinks that if she were perfect, you would not want anyone else. To "want" someone else in this sense can mean paying attention to someone, spending time with another person, admiring something about a person, and so on.

Putting Your Needs First

Does your partner frequently subjugate her needs or desires in favor of yours? Think about it. Examples of subjugating her needs or desires, can take the following forms. Does she

- fix only the food or menus that you like?

- let you select the television programs the two of you watch?

- only attend social events you select and attend with her?

- make sure that you get the newest clothes or fashions?

- try to save money by not buying things for herself so that you will have more to spend?

- delay medical and dental medical treatment in order to make more money available for you?

If many or all of these reflect your partner's behavior most of the time, then she is most likely trying to take care of you so well that you would never consider abandoning or destroying her. Her intent is to make your life so comfortable, and cause you to feel so special, that you will be grateful and appreciative of her sacrifices; you would feel guilty or ashamed if you were to leave or if you were attracted to someone else.

The mutuality in a relationship involves putting each other's needs and desires first at times. That is, there are times when each of you will need to take precedence for resources, preferences, services, and so on. The quality of the relationship can be seen in the partners' willingness to take care of each other, alternating so that neither partner is very frequently subjugating her needs in favor of the other partner. Is your relationship characterized by mutuality, or do your needs, wants, and desires most often receive preference?

The payoff for always subjugating her needs is that it sets up a debt that you can never fully pay. If this behavior characterizes your partner, she most likely learned this role and expectation at an early age when she was expected to subjugate her needs to a parent's needs, wishes, and desires. That did not get her the attention, admiration, and love she sought then, and it is not getting her what she wants now, but she does not know any other way to behave, nor is she aware of why she behaves as she does.

Seeking Fusion and Enmeshment

Your clingy partner may be seeking fusion and enmeshment with you, but she is not aware of what she is doing. She only knows that when she is not with you she feels lonely, isolated, adrift, afraid, disconnected, and incomplete, like a part of her is missing.

I don't mean that she feels this way when you are away for an extended period of time, such as an extended business trip. No, she feels this way every time you leave the house or, in extreme cases, when you are not in the same room with her. She may need your presence so much that you seldom, if ever, have a moment to yourself to work on a hobby, read, or just sit and think.

This need for fusion and enmeshment stems from poor boundary strength; your partner has not yet adequately completed the developmental tasks of separation and individuation. Separation means that she can perceive herself as a separate and distinct person, and she can also be aware of others as unique persons. Individuation means that she has developed her own self-identity, and her attitudes, values, and beliefs were freely chosen by her, although they continue to carry early-life, parental, and familial influences. Fusion and enmeshment with another person are the only ways she knows to keep herself from disappearing.

Just think about some romantic phrases that support the notion that romantic and intimate partners should be fused or enmeshed:

- Two hearts that beat as one.
- You never see one without the other.
- I'm a part of you, and you're part of me.
- I'm lost whenever you are away.
- I can't live without you.
- You are the only one for me.
- I am nothing without you.

Partners who have not yet developed an integrated and cohesive self may need the other person in order to feel complete and whole. Thus any threat to that completeness and wholeness is a threat to the essential self, which must be defended at all costs.

Hypersensitivity

People who are hypersensitive to perceived criticism stay in a defensive mode. They see criticism where no criticism was meant. They feel that others are constantly expecting them to take care of them, fix whatever needs fixing, maintain harmony, and so on, and they also feel blamed when things don't go right. They feel this way even when the feeling isn't realistic, rational, or responsible. They are at the mercy of some irrational and faulty assumptions tinged with grandiosity, so that they assume they are powerful enough to do these things.

The hypersensitive partner can easily take offense at implied criticism or blame, assume you are being critical or blaming when you don't say anything, expect compliments and appreciation for almost everything she does, become profoundly disappointed and self-critical when you don't seem pleased with almost everything she does, or think that she has failed when you are in a bad mood or just want some space. These characteristics, attitudes, and feelings can keep you in a constant state of tension because you may do, or fail to do, something that sets off her perception that you are blaming her.

Your partner's hypersensitivity may be the result of being a "parentified" child, who was expected to take care of her parent's emotional and psychological well-being. Also at work are some old parental messages of blame for not being perfect, for not preventing the parent from feeling discomfort, and so on. It is from experiences like these that she developed the faulty assumptions that she is responsible when you feel distress or discomfort, that you blame her for your discomfort and distress, that she is not good enough to prevent your discomfort or distress, and that you will abandon her because of these inadequacies.

Feelings Being Easily Hurt

Does just about everything you say seem to produce hurt feelings in your partner? Are you constantly soothing your partner or apologizing for hurting her feelings? Do you feel that your partner tends to take too much as a personal attack? If so, then your partner may have one or more of the following conditions:

- insufficient boundary strength to defend the self

- the notion that she will be abandoned and destroyed if she makes a mistake or is not good enough

- the fear that her self is inadequate

- the need for control and reassurance

- a learned behavior or habit of manipulating others

- lack of self-confidence and self-efficacy

- wanting attention, admiration, or to be considered special

- considerable self-absorption

Think of your early adolescence, when everything was dramatic, you were searching for your self-identity, and everyone seemed to be trying to tell you how inadequate you were. During that period you may have had your feelings hurt on a regular basis, not always by the same person. This is what is known in the psychological literature as *narcissistic wounding,* a hurt to the essential or core self, and this hurt can be what your partner is experiencing. When narcissistic wounding occurs, the person is so hurt that nothing really makes it heal or go away. And just about everything seems to reopen the wound or to touch that sensitive spot, all on the unconscious level. The original hurt occurred early in life and was not worked through, so now the self is not sufficiently strong, healthy, and defended.

If this is what is happening in your partner, there is little or nothing you can do to help her develop a stronger self, better boundaries, and more confidence. Her feelings will continue to be easily hurt, neither of you will understand why or how to stop it, and the relationship may be affected.

The discussion has focused on identifying the "clingy" style of jealousy. If many of these described behaviors and attitudes seem to fit your partner, then she may indeed be "clingy." You must remember that many of these aspects were part of what attracted you to her in the first place, are an integral part of your partner, and are most likely subject only to moderate modification. Chapter

8 presents some specific and general suggestions to help you cope with your clingy partner.

The Reactive Jealous Partner

The reactive jealous partner could also be termed "paranoid" or "suspicious." She is almost the opposite of the clingy partner in many ways. For example, where the clingy person is overattentive, trying to meet unexpressed needs, the reactive partner relies on you to constantly and openly express your needs and may insist that you provide more information. The clingy partner may try to arouse your guilt and shame as a defense, whereas the reactive partner is more likely to attack and go on the offensive.

Scale 2: The Reactive Jealous Partner Scale

Use the following scale to rate your partner's reactive behaviors, attitudes, and feelings.

5—always, or almost always
4—frequently
3—sometimes
2—seldom
1—never, or almost never

1. Your partner appears edgy, tense, and anxious.	
2. Your partner wants or demands to know everything you think, feel, or do.	
3. Your partner seems suspicious of all your actions, activities, friends, and so on.	
4. Your partner attacks you and others by using sarcasm, put-downs, and other criticizing remarks.	
5. Your partner blames you for how she feels.	
6. Your partner is suspicious and skeptical about others' interests and motives.	

7. Your partner exaggerates what she perceives as signs of your desire to leave, alienation of your affection, and the like.	
8. Your partner stays on guard and does not seem to relax.	
9. Your partner holds grudges and cannot let go of negative thoughts and reactions.	

Scoring

Add the ratings to get a total score. A rating of 41 to 50 indicates considerable reactivity and suspicion; 31 to 40 indicates many behaviors indicative of reactivity; 21 to 30 indicates some of these; 11 to 20 indicates few such behaviors, attitudes, and feelings; and 0 to 10 indicates almost none of these.

Edginess, Tension, and Anxiety

Your partner may be a very intense person. You may have initially interpreted her intensity as energy, focus, determination, and passion, especially if you tended to be the opposite. You may have been attached to her decisiveness, intense interest, and ability to maintain a focus. It was only later that you began to realize the flip sides of these attractive characteristics in your partner were edginess, a constant state of tension, and anxiety. That edginess, tension, and anxiety can make life very uncomfortable for you at times, because you can catch these feelings without meaning to.

This is a person who is always alert to signs of danger to the self. That alertness translates into edginess and tension and a constant state of preparedness to fight or flee from danger. Just because the potential danger is psychological, and not physical, does not lessen the impact on the person. Her physical, psychological, emotional, and relational selves are all affected, and that effect is usually negative. For example, the edgy, tense, and anxious person can develop chronic physical health conditions such as hypertension, and psychological concerns such as intrusive thoughts. And her relationships can be affected, since others are uncomfortable when they have to interact with the person over a period of time.

If this describes your partner, you may find that you seek some relief from her intensity by withdrawing or by interacting with others. Whatever you do, however, can be perceived as a rejection of her, and her jealousy gets aroused. You don't consciously seek the relief—it is not necessarily deliberate on your part, but your partner may think that it is. Since she is already in a high state of alert to potential abandonment or destruction, she is always ready to think that the danger is imminent and real. You cannot convince her otherwise.

Wanting to Know Everything

Your partner's desire to know everything you do, think, and feel is a part of her alertness to potential danger. Your partner believes that she can take care of her self and prevent you from abandoning her by knowing everything about you. That way she can do something to prevent the feared thing from happening.

Your partner may also feel that your choice to not tell her everything is a deliberate attempt on your part to mislead her into thinking that your relationship is fine even though you really don't think things are okay and don't want her to know. Has your partner made any of the following statements, or similar comments, on a regular or frequent basis?

- I don't know you at all.

- You never tell me anything about what's going on with you.

- Why are you so secretive? I tell you everything about my day, but you don't tell me anything about yours.

- I never know what you are thinking.

- After all this time together, I still can't predict what you will do.

- You keep everything to yourself.

- I feel left out of your life. You don't tell me anything.

- You don't want me to know what you are doing.

Even when you try to give your partner more information, she remains suspicious because it is not possible to tell her everything she wants to know. And even if you could tell her everything, she would always think that there was something you were keeping back. She can never be satisfied that she knows everything about you and thus remains convinced that she is in danger of being abandoned or destroyed. Notice the shift here. The focus has changed from being about you to being about her. That is the crux of the problem. Your partner feels she is in danger and believes that knowing all about you—which is not possible—can prevent the danger from affecting her.

Some people, possibly including your partner, think that asking many questions shows interest on their part. However, there are a number of people whose reaction to questioning is to feel attacked. This feeling can be especially acute when they are bombarded with many questions. If this latter description fits you, and the former fits your partner, you two may want to clarify your perceptions with each other. For example, when your partner asks you many questions, you can ask her if she is trying to show interest or is suspicious of something. This may seem a little direct, but you get the idea.

It could be that your partner tells you everything and is expecting you to do the same in return. Again, you two may want to clarify your expectations of each other. Your partner may feel uneasy and anxious when you don't tell her everything but perhaps she can learn to tolerate some anxiety if she is confident that you are not deliberately hiding anything important to the relationship. That is, her fear that you are abandoning her physically, emotionally, or psychologically would be reduced.

Suspicion

If there is one word that is descriptive of a reactive jealous partner, that word would be *suspicious*. She suspects that something is going on that she doesn't know about, and believes that thing is a threat to her and to the relationship. While this suspicion may be valid in her other relationships, many times she is seeing a threat where no threat exists.

You may wonder why your partner is so suspicious of everything you do and the people in your life. Take a look at the chapters on past experiences and family of origin factors. Your partner most likely has experienced many of the events described there, and these have deeply affected her. Her inner world is not a safe one, and her external experiences have added to her feelings of threat and danger. She has probably experienced one or more of the following:

- being betrayed by someone she trusted

- being rejected

- discovering that her parents lied to her and, subsequently, that others lied to her

- seeing others being betrayed and the effect on them

- reading about the misconduct of public officials who have betrayed the trusting public

- hearing, reading, or discovering that lies were invented about someone

- observing cheating and stealing in everyday life

- being told not to trust

These are experiences that are not unique to your partner. They are common; just about everyone has experienced several of them. However, your partner was hurt and made to feel foolish and inadequate at an early age by betrayal, rejection, or lies. This was very wounding to her developing self, and that hurt persists today. She has discovered that if she maintains some skepticism and suspicion, she is less likely to be surprised and hurt by someone's actions. It is not so much that she always wants to hear or see the truth; she is simply doing what she can to not be misled, jerked around, taken advantage of, and hurt. None of these is your intent, but her suspicious nature is deeply ingrained.

Attacking Behaviors

People who use sarcasm, put-downs, and constant criticisms are using these to defend the self from shame, guilt, fear of not being good enough, feeling inferior, and being attacked.

Hurtful words are often intended to keep others on the defensive, to illustrate the speaker's superiority, and to maintain power and control.

Sarcasm is often thought to be humor, but in reality it is a wounding, attacking behavior that is meant to keep others off balance and prevent retaliation. If you object to being the target of sarcasm, you may then be told that you "can't take a joke." Humor that hurts is not real or appropriate humor; it is a weapon. If your partner often uses sarcasm with you, she is not being funny—she is attacking you.

Put-downs are easily perceived as attempts to show the other person as inferior and highlight the speaker's superiority. The person's achievements are minimized, personal qualities denigrated, and other characteristics diminished. The person who uses put-downs fears that she is not adequate; she has a need to feel superior and so uses this method to attain what she needs.

Constant criticism can represent either a need for perfection or an attempt to feel adequate by pointing out others' inadequacies, or both. If your jealous partner constantly criticizes you and others (it's seldom that a constant criticizer targets just one person), she is probably fearful that she will be unmasked as inadequate, and so she defends against that possible event by attacking you and others.

Attacks like these are indirect and difficult for the receiver to defend against. They are easier to understand and ignore if you can remember that your partner is actually very fearful and is using these to defend herself against the fear.

Blaming

The reactive partner can also be very blaming. She seems to think that it is never her fault when things don't go as planned—it is your inadequacy or deliberate actions that are the cause—and she isn't shy in making you aware of this. Your partner may be the kind of person who believes she is never wrong, off-loads blame and responsibility whenever possible, and can find multiple reasons why she is not at fault even when she has sole and total responsibility for what happened.

People who fit this description feel deeply wounded whenever it appears that they are not good enough, inadequate, at fault, and the like. This wounding occurs as a result of family of origin experiences in early life, especially old parental messages. She is still reacting to these even though she is an adult. She has not moved from the polarities of "I'm all good" or "I'm all bad" to the more rational and integrated "I'm reasonably good but have some flaws and inadequacies." She continues to reject unacceptable parts of her self and project them onto you and others.

This behavior represents a fear of being found out as inadequate and flawed, which she believes would lead to you rejecting and abandoning her. It's ironic that the very behavior she uses to ward off this fear—blame—is one that just might bring about what she fears most: the person who constantly receives blame can become hurt, resentful, and angry and finally decide that it is not beneficial or worthwhile to continue to stay in a relationship where he is constantly blamed.

Your partner's blaming can extend to her jealousy: she may blame you for causing her to feel this way. You did something, or did not do something, that led her to become jealous. If you were "better" you would not "make" her jealous. She ignores or is unaware of the fact that her feelings are her responsibility, that she attached the meaning to your actions or nonactions, and that you did not make her jealous.

Suspicion and Skepticism about Others' Motives

It may seem that your partner believes the worst about other people, and this can become an issue between you. Not only does she fear that you are poised to give your affections away to someone else, but she also seems convinced that almost everyone else is trying to steal your affections. Nothing you say or do seems to make a dent in her perception.

This suspiciousness and skepticism extends to other parts of her life, where she views others' motives as questionable. To your partner, nothing is as it appears to be. She believes that others' motives are not benign, good, or trustworthy, because these people are doing the following:

- seeking to take advantage

- looking out for their own needs

- trying to manipulate and control

- showing that they are more powerful

- putting you at a disadvantage

- trying to get what you have

- taking something away from you

This perception of others is a very dismal one, which you may not share. You may be more trusting and accepting, and less judgmental, and her perceptions can be upsetting to you at times.

Your partner gained this perspective from her past experiences when she trusted someone only to be betrayed, not realizing until too late that she was being manipulated and doing things she did not want to do. She may have felt foolish for trusting or believing in someone only to find out that they were deceiving her, lost a relationship that was valuable, or had other similar negative experiences. Suspicion and skepticism are learned attitudes, just as your partner may have learned very well the potential costs of trusting and relying on others. The fact that you are different and are trustworthy does not mean that she will be able to let go of her deeply felt suspicion and skepticism. She has more evidence of the negative effects of not being suspicious and skeptical than she has evidence of the positive effects for being trusting, open, accepting, and nonjudgmental. These attitudes are her protection from hurt, rejection, feeling foolish, being betrayed, or being manipulated. Your relationship may develop to the point where she trusts you more, but she may never allow herself to completely trust anyone nor bring herself to be less suspicious and skeptical of others.

Exaggeration

Does your jealous partner exaggerate what you do or say, or what someone else does or says, when her jealousy gets aroused? That is, would she take a casual conversation you had with someone and describe it as intimate? Or would she take use your late arrival as an indication that you must have found the person with whom you were meeting to be engaging, or you would not have been late? Or would she imply that if you really loved her you would do, or not do, whatever it is that she objects to? You can probably think of some situations on your own that illustrate her tendency to exaggerate.

If you protest that her description of you is an exaggeration, she gets upset and enraged. Before you know it, the two of you are having an argument, or you've stomped off to cool down. The conflict has moved from being about what you did or did not do or say to your partner's defense of her description. In addition, she may think that you raised the objection just to get her off the subject. This is a no-win situation.

People who are prone to exaggerate seem to have difficulty with ambiguity and gradations. They seem to perceive the world in general, all-or-nothing terms, such as *always* and *never*. For example, they don't comprehend that a mild flirting glance at someone else does not mean that you are attracted and will leave them. They don't accept that you can like someone without being ready to love that person. Any explanation you provide of your feelings or behavior that is not defensive is seen by your partner as an attempt to mislead her, defend you, and be untruthful. Many times this leads to a fight.

You may need to accept your partner's tendency to exaggerate and not let the exaggeration upset you. It could be more helpful to listen to her underlying message and try to overlook her exaggerations. The tendency to exaggerate is very much like what children do. I remember a time when I asked my three children, ages five, seven, and ten, what happened to a package of cookies I had just bought, which was now empty. They said, "Papa ate all the cookies." This seemed strange to me, since he did not usually do this. So I asked my husband why he ate all the cookies. His response was that he had eaten one cookie, the last one. The children translated his eating the last cookie into his eating all of the cookies. You can probably think of similar stories about children's tendency to exaggerate, and those stories may be similar to things your partner has said or done.

Inability to Relax

This tendency is similar to edginess, discussed earlier in this chapter, but it is somewhat different. There may not be constant tension, but your partner seems to remain in a state of guardedness where she seems cautious, tentative, and fearful of being hurt almost all the time. Her guardedness keeps you in a state of tension in which you hardly know what to do or say for fear of inflicting hurt. You then become cautious and tentative yourself, which can be very uncomfortable for you and is not helpful for the relationship.

By this time you probably have no trouble understanding that your partner's family of origin experiences and other past experiences play major roles in her behavior and attitudes. She probably does not consciously realize what she is doing, why she is doing it, nor the impact on you. Even when you try to bring it to her attention, she does not let go of this defensive posture. She is defensive because of deep, enduring, painful experiences. As a result, she perceives the world as a hostile place filled with people who intend to hurt her, and she cannot imagine that others are not having the same experiences and reactions. This stance has afforded her some protection, but it has not changed her basic view of herself, and of her world. You may make some headway at changing this, but you probably can do very little.

Your partner's jealousy is easily aroused because she has a pessimistic outlook on herself and her relationships. She fears that she is not competent, effective, or powerful enough to prevent others from hurting her, and this translates to her being constantly on guard to do whatever she can to keep from being deeply hurt and disappointed one more time. She may trust you more than anyone else in her life, but that does not mean that she trusts you very much at all. She is expecting hurt and disappointment, but by not trusting you she unwittingly acts in such a way as to foster the hurt and disappointment she dreads. When the very thing she fears does indeed happen, she is not terribly surprised.

Holding Grudges

Your partner may engage in several of the following behaviors and attitudes:

- seems to obsess over the slightest event that was upsetting or troubling to her

- holds a grudge for a very long time or forever

- cannot relinquish hurt feelings

- seethes internally, and then explodes over a minor event

- tends to categorize people as all good or all bad

- perceives people who have offended her once as forever poised to do it again

- keeps the offense as clear and bright in her mind as it was when it occurred

- seems to find it difficult to accept apologies

Your partner may also engage in circular or spiral thinking: a person, event, or feeling leads to other similar events that only intensify the negative thoughts and feelings. She then cannot get out of the circle and may spiral down into depression.

She may also engage in all-or-nothing thinking. To her, people's actions and other events are not happenstance, a one-time event, or a lapse in good judgment. Rather, she thinks of these as all good or all bad, with no in between. For example, even though someone offended her when both were adolescents and somewhat self-absorbed, she continues to carry a grudge against that person, even though a more adult perspective should allow her to see the offense for what is was—an insensitive act by an adolescent. However, she continues to perceive that person as she did when both were teens and cannot move to a more adult perspective.

The items in the list above are examples of narcissistic wounding—situations where the core or essential self has been hurt and has not healed. After someone has received a narcissistic wound, it does not take much to reopen old hurts and relive some of the wounding experiences. It can get to the point where the person expects to be wounded, and can access these old hurts easily at any time. This hypersensitivity can be very hard on relationships and is difficult to overcome.

The person with a "reactive" style is very fearful of losing the relationship and of not being good enough for her partner to want to stay with her. She is constantly on the alert and reads signs and portents into everything, and it is almost impossible to convince her that she is basically a lovable person. Her earlier life experiences do not permit her to trust anyone for fear of once more being deeply hurt. While you get irritated at her jealousy and suspicions, she is locked in her fear of being abandoned or destroyed.

Chapter 7

The Jealous Partner: Manipulative and Exhibitionistic Styles

This chapter discusses the manipulative and exhibitionistic styles of jealousy. These styles can be more troubling to the relationship and destructive to your self-esteem than the clingy and paranoid styles. They are more troubling because they are more difficult to identify, especially at the beginning of a relationship. It usually takes some time before you realize what is happening, and you can experience considerable distress during that time. Some of the behaviors and attitudes displayed by partners with these styles are also corrosive to your self-esteem. You may experience a sense of failure or inadequacy not only because of your unresolved issues but also because your partner is doing and saying things designed to erode your self-confidence.

The Manipulative Style

The manipulative jealous partner can be sneaky, underhanded, and double crossing. You are never sure if what you see is really him, or if he is using smoke and mirrors to present an illusion and confuse you. There may even have been times he faked being jealous so that you would be put in a position where he could more easily manipulate you.

Scale 3: The Manipulative Jealous Partner Scale

Use the following scale to rate your partner's behaviors and attitudes.

5—always, or almost always
4—frequently
3—sometimes
2—seldom
1—never, or almost never

1. Your partner lies, distorts, and misleads.	
2. Your partner can be charming when caught lying or cheating.	
3. Your partner is able to con or persuade you to do things that you do not want to do or are not in your best interest.	
4. Your partner has been known to "set you up" so that he can express his jealousy.	
5. Your partner indirectly expresses jealousy.	
6. Your partner puts you on the defensive by making accusations he knows are not true.	
7. Your partner deliberately does and says things to make you feel inadequate.	
8. Your partner behaves in such a way as to demonstrate his power and control over you.	
9. Your partner manipulates disagreements so that you wind up being in the wrong or at fault.	
10. Your partner cheats.	

Scoring

Add the ratings for a score. A rating of 41 to 50 indicates that your partner is extremely manipulative; 31 to 40 indicates that he is very manipulative; 21 to 30 indicates that he can be manipulative at times; 11 to 20 indicates that he occasionally uses a little manipulation; and 0 to 10 indicates that he seldom or never uses manipulation. If the score is below 30, you may be unaware of your partner's manipulative behaviors and attitudes. It can be easy to defend, rationalize, or excuse what he does in your effort to avoid feeling manipulated. You may want to review your answers with this in mind, to make sure you are not trying to explain away some manipulative behaviors and attitudes.

Deception and Distortion

Perhaps you believe that lying, distorting, and misleading are not characteristic behaviors of your partner. You may think he does not do these with you, just with other people. However, you can be sure that if he lies, distorts, or misleads when dealing with others, he does the same with you; you are just not letting yourself know this, or he is able to hide it from you. Either way, you can be unpleasantly surprised one day when the lies and distortions are revealed.

Why does your partner lie, distort, or try to mislead? He may do this for any or all of the following reasons:

- to make himself appear superior and powerful
- to put others on the defensive
- to cover up feelings of inferiority or of not being good enough
- to manipulate and control others
- to hide his misdeeds and misconduct
- to mask shame and guilt

The items in the list are inner states that have their roots in his family of origin experiences, and in some of his past experiences. His self-concept may be so shaky and inadequate that the only way he can feel adequate is by lying, distorting the truth, and misleading.

You are not immune to his behavior and attitudes. He may feel that he is entitled to do whatever he needs to feel adequate, powerful, and in control, and this extends to you. You think that you have not experienced his lying, distracting, and misleading, but you may be turning a blind eye or choosing to overlook these behaviors. The manipulative person is manipulative with everyone.

There are three major goals for this behavior: to get something from another person, to feel superior, and to shore up the self. The first is overt, direct, and known to the person doing the manipulating. He knows what he intends to accomplish by his deception. The second is also known to him, but it may be on a nonconscious level. He may deny it, but he gets satisfaction from "putting one over." The third is unconscious. He does not realize that his needs to feel adequate, good enough, and acceptable are the basis of this deceptive behavior. These goals, along with his entitlement attitude, contribute to his constant lying, misleading, and distorting.

Charm

People who tend to frequently lie, distort, mislead, and cheat are not always successful at this. They do get caught. But one reason they persist in these behaviors is that they are able to charm their way out of the situation. They are able to explain it away, flatter the catcher, deflect irate feelings, or minimize what they did. Your partner may use his charm whenever he feels he is in danger of your learning about, understanding, or objecting to his manipulation of you.

If your partner's style is manipulative, his jealousy will tend to be expressed in indirect ways. He can tell you things about the target of his jealousy that are designed to get you to reject that person or persons, including relatives, friends, and acquaintances. Think about it: Has your partner lied, made misleading comments about someone, or distorted what someone said or did, and you believed him? Did you start to reject or withdraw from that person because of what your partner told you? Did you challenge your partner when you found out the truth, only to be charmed away from your annoyance or anger? If so, you may want to consider that you are being manipulated.

Some people seem to be born with considerable charm, and many people are attracted to them. Almost everyone can appreciate charming people and may even want to be just as charming. It is not that charming people are not sincere, as many are. However, some people use charm as a way to wiggle out of uncomfortable situations, to con people, and to demonstrate their power and control. You will have to decide whether this description fits your partner, whether you can develop some immunity to his charm for your own protection, and how you can stay more aware of what he is doing when he seeks to charm you.

Conning and Persuasion

It can be disconcerting to frequently find yourself doing things you do not want to do, or acting contrary to your best interests. You may even resolve not to let this happen again, only to realize that you have let it happen and that you don't seem to be able to stop it. This can be particularly distressing when it is your partner who puts you in this position, seemingly at will.

He is able to con or persuade you because of the nature of an intimate relationship, and because you may lack some boundary strength. These two reasons are interrelated and complex and cannot be fully explained here. The nature of an intimate relationship demands that partners lower their defenses, be open and accessible, try to empathize with each other, and connect at a deep level.

In order to be intimate, your psychological boundaries have to let your partner in. If you have the desired strong and resilient boundaries, you can do this without becoming enmeshed or overwhelmed. You never lose your sense of yourself as a separate and distinct person. If, on the other hand, you lack some boundary strength or development, you can become enmeshed, so that you cannot distinguish between you and the other person, and begin to adopt his perspective and attitude, which can lead to your doing what he wants you to do. Or, you can become overwhelmed, so that he can take over and direct you to act as he wishes you to act. What is most troubling about all of this is that it takes place on a nonconscious or unconscious level, and you remain unaware of what is happening until it is too late. My book *Whose Life Is It Anyway? When to Stop Taking Care of Their Feelings and Start Taking Care of Your Own* (Brown 2002) describes this process and gives suggestions for building strong and resilient boundaries.

Setting You Up

Your partner may be the kind of person who gets a kick out of setting people up to make them appear foolish, set the scene for a jealous tantrum, put them at a disadvantage, highlight their inferiority, take the blame for a misdeed, or just for fun.

The person who is set up doesn't realize what is happening at the time, may never realize or accept that he was set up, but still suffers the consequences or outcomes. The manipulative person who engineered the setup can be pleased and gratified at his success, laugh behind the person's back or even to his face, and assure himself of his superiority at being able to bring it off.

If this description does fit your jealous partner, he is working hard to overcome his unconscious suspicions that he is inferior, not good enough, unlovable, and unacceptable. It is only when he can manipulate others into compromising positions that he can reject these suspicions about himself. Sadly, his relationships are being used, abused, and sacrificed in defense of himself.

What could be examples of possible setups by a jealous partner?

- inviting someone he thinks is a potential rival to your home for dinner, and showing up very late

- being suspicious of someone and making sure that you are often alone with that person

- inviting you and someone he suspects you like for lunch or dinner, and watching you closely as you interact with the person

- not showing up for the show, dinner, or other outing where his suspected rival is supposed to join the two of you

- doing and saying things to make you think he likes the rival and wants you to like him too, but becoming upset when you agree

Indirect Expressions of Jealousy

The partner with a manipulative style will seldom if ever directly express his jealousy. He tends to try and manipulate you into expressing his fear and anger so that he can appear to remain calm and in control. You are then put at a disadvantage; you are blamed for whatever aroused his jealousy, and you are criticized when you express fear and anger. This is most frustrating, and if you are innocent of whatever your partner believes you are doing, or are unaware of what he is thinking, you can find yourself feeling hurt and enraged, and *you don't know why!* The preceding phrase is italicized because you are probably bewildered and confused, in addition to all your other feelings. You are caught in a maelstrom and don't have a clue as to what is going on, how you got to this place, or how to find your way out.

What can be happening is that you are catching your partner's feelings, identifying with all or parts of them, and then acting on them. For example, your partner may be angry, does not want or accept his anger, and projects it on you; you catch the projected anger, incorporate it into yourself, and then become angry and express the combined anger. He has gotten rid of his anger, but you are angry, and you don't understand why.

Projecting his feelings onto you or others is only one way your partner can indirectly express his jealousy. Some other ways include

- criticizing the target of his jealousy

- criticizing you

- making sarcastic and demeaning remarks about you or the other person

- becoming more needy

- refusing to be soothed or placated

- sinking into a depression

- sulking and withdrawing

- displacing the feelings on someone else

- attempting to retaliate by trying to make you jealous

It can take a long time for you to recognize signs of your partner's jealousy, because he expresses it in indirect ways. This also makes it difficult for you to address it, because trying to meet it head on will allow him to deny it. Either way, you lose.

False Accusations

If your partner has a manipulative style, he may like to "stir the pot." That is, he will make false accusations just to see what you will do or say. He knows that the accusations have no validity, but he puts them forward as if he really believes them. Most of the time he convinces you that he believes them, but there may be times when you wonder if he could possibly believe what he charges. You don't want to think that he would deliberately accuse you falsely, because you don't want to believe he could be so hurtful and destructive.

A manipulative partner works to do the following:

- keep you off balance

- do and say things designed to make you edgy, cautious, and tentative

- try to convince you that he has your best interests at heart

- fuel his need for power and control

- reassure himself that he is superior

- put you on the defensive

- hide and mask his real self

Making false accusations is an effective way to accomplish what he works hard to achieve. When you are falsely accused you can become edgy, tense, and off balance. And, while you don't want to think that he is deriving satisfaction and pleasure from your discomfort, he may very well be doing just that.

What can he gain from making these false accusations? There are several possibilities. First, you are on the defensive trying to answer the unanswerable. The more you try to explain or refute the charges, the worse your position becomes, and you know it. At some point he will accept what you say, and your relief is so great that you don't try to get at what he really believes. Second, he is gaining power and control over you and the relationship. You can become skittish and edgy, fearing additional accusations at any time. Third, he succeeds at putting you in an inferior position, thereby reassuring himself of his superiority. Fourth, he derives a feeling of glee from getting away with making these false accusations. He can be very confident and satisfied with his self-worth when he succeeds.

Attempts to Make You Feel Inadequate

Another tactic of manipulative people is to say and do things that are intended to make you feel inadequate. When you feel inadequate, the accompanying guilt and shame lead you to try to get rid of these feelings or to compensate for them in some way. Your jealous partner understands how this works and uses it to his advantage. It's a form of revenge for the hurt and inadequacy he feels when his jealousy is aroused.

For example, suppose you and your partner are attending your child's soccer game at a local recreation field. You talk with several other parents there, but your partner thinks you are flirting with one of the parents. When you try to start a conversation with your partner, he mentions that he noticed that your shorts are tighter than they were a month ago, and that the backs of your thighs show some cellulite. When you look at him in dismay, he shrugs and says that he just thought you would want to know so that you could do something about it. He has probably succeeded in making you feel inadequate. You'll be more vulnerable to his other manipulative tactics because you are still caught up in your feelings over your appearance.

Due to the intimate nature of the relationship, there are many situations and ways your partner can make you feel inadequate. You've told him about some of your insecurities and sensitivities, he can see some that you don't, and he can guess at some that are very well hidden. He has a range of topics to choose from that can trigger your feelings of inadequacy. The important thing for you to remember in these instances is that you are in charge of how you feel. Even though someone is trying to make you feel inadequate, you do not have to feel that way. For example, in the situation at the soccer game, you have a variety of emotional responses you could choose:

- You could act amused.

- You could disregard his comment and be accepting of your physical self.

- You could be puzzled by his comment.

- You could feel that he doesn't love you anymore.

You could respond in any of the following ways:

- You could sigh and say that this means an end to your modeling career.

- You could say, "Really," as if you are unconcerned.

- Or you could ignore the comment and not respond at all (my personal favorite).

If you refuse to buy into the manipulation and feel inadequate, he loses.

Demonstrations of Power and Control

Face it: when you love someone, that person does have some power and control over you, and your hope is that he will not misuse this power. You cannot love someone without giving him the ability to affect you deeply. The nature of love and intimacy is characterized by your vulnerability to each other, whether the relationship is with a child, parent, or lover. There is power and control in every relationship, and the distribution of these factors is not equal between the two of you at any given time (although it may be equal in the long run).

When your manipulative, jealous partner feels inadequate, not good enough, at a disadvantage, in danger of having feelings of inferiority emerge, or potential shame if others would see his inadequacies, he can be motivated to demonstrate his control and power over you. He does this to ward off the negative feelings and reassure himself of his superiority and competence. He moves quickly to make it clear who is in charge in the relationship.

There are many ways to demonstrate power and control. Your partner may

- become more needy
- start to whine and complain
- tell you that you are being insensitive
- become openly affectionate with you
- start being openly affectionate with someone else
- pointedly ignore you
- refuse a request, such as saying no when you want to go home
- create an embarrassing scene

- start a fight

- tell you to do something or to stop doing something in a commanding voice

- give you orders

Manipulation of Disagreements

It can be frustrating and infuriating to end up in the "wrong" in almost every disagreement, and you may wonder how this happens. You start out secure and confident in your perspective, opinion, or argument, but somehow the situation gets turned around so that you end up losing. You seldom leave a disagreement with your partner without feeling upset, angry, confused, and anxious. Disagreements with your partner seldom clear the air, tending instead to make things even more tense and uncomfortable. The person with a manipulative style is a master of this technique.

What generally happens is that you have an emotional investment in the disagreement, no matter how minor the disagreement may be. Your partner senses this, or he knows you so well that he can count on your being emotionally invested. Your emotional investment means that you care about your position and about the outcome of the argument. It also means that you are not able to clearly see what is taking place, because you are operating more on the feeling level than on the thinking or analytical level. You are open to your partner's emotional "sending," and so you can catch some of his more negative feelings, such as guilt, shame, and anger. Once you get in touch with any of these feelings, irrational or not, your partner can manipulate you into expressing these, and then very rationally point out how wrong you are. The sending and catching of feelings takes place on a nonconscious or unconscious level, but his words or actions may contribute to your feelings. You are caught in the grip of emotions while he stays free from them—he will win every time.

Your partner may also be the kind of person who never forgets any mistakes or errors you make and generalizes these to everything you do or say. He brings them up frequently, just to put you at a disadvantage. This strategy can be particularly effective if you are still embarrassed, humiliated, guilty, or have shame around a particular event. Your partner does this to show that your inferiority and inadequacy extend to almost everything in your life. No matter how much you try to stay focused on the present disagreement, he brings old disagreements or mistakes into the present one. This is another form of manipulation to keep you at a disadvantage and in the "wrong."

Cheating Behavior

Cheating can include the following behaviors and attitudes:

- taking unfair advantage

- betrayal of trust

- contempt for the other person in the relationship

- a need to demonstrate personal superiority and adequacy

- an attitude of entitlement

- trying to "put something over" on the other person

- a lack of commitment to the relationship

- arrogance ("I will not get caught")

Cheating is not limited to intimacy outside the current relationship, which can be very troubling. Cheating can actually occur in every aspect of the person's life, whether it is work or play, and with family, friends, and people he does not know. For example, in the news we see cheating in high-ranking people ranging from CEOs and government officials to religious leaders.

Your manipulative partner uses cheating and the potential for cheating as weapons to get you to do what he wants you to do. Your fear and dread of losing him and the relationship allow you to buy into the manipulation. You may find yourself rationalizing your discomfort with doing what you don't want to do or what is not in your best interests. However, you are in charge of your feelings, and you have to decide what you are willing to accept from your partner, and what you will not accept.

This characteristic, like the others in this discussion about the manipulative style, illustrates the slyness, deceitfulness, and arrogance of those who have this style. They also have an overlay of charm that allows them to operate as they do and not suffer many consequences for their behavior and attitudes. A relationship with someone who has this style can be uncomfortable for reasons that are invisible to you. The manipulation can be well hidden; a great deal of it takes place on the nonconscious and unconscious levels.

The Exhibitionistic Style

This style has behavior and characteristics that are intended to illustrate the person's grandness and superiority, arouse envy, garner attention and admiration, solicit deference from others, and emphasize his unique and special qualities.

This style is a showy one that keeps the person at the center of attention. It differs from the clingy style, since this person does not keep you at the center of his attention; rather he expects you and others to keep him at the center of their attention. The person with a clingy style is trying to hold onto your affections with overconcern and overattentiveness. The person with an exhibitionistic style assumes he is at the center of your interest and affection, and he expects you to constantly demonstrate it.

Scale 4: Exhibitionistic Jealous Partner	
Use the following scale to determine if your partner has an exhibitionistic style. 5—always, or almost always 4—frequently 3—sometimes 2—seldom 1—never, or almost never	
1. Your partner shows off (physical appearance, possessions, etc.).	
2. Your partner has to have the biggest or best of everything.	
3. Your partner boasts and brags at every opportunity.	
4. Your partner tries to take unearned credit.	

5. Your partner expects you to suppress your needs, wants, and desires in favor of his.	
6. Your partner becomes upset when he feels he is being ignored or overlooked.	
7. Your partner acts to get attention.	
8. Your partner fishes for compliments, flattery, and the like.	
9. Your partner expects others to show him that they recognize and appreciate his superiority.	
10. Your partner does not seem to understand how other people feel.	

Scoring

Add your ratings to derive a total score. A score of 41 to 50 indicates a severe exhibitionistic style; 31 to 40 indicates a frequent exhibitionistic style; 21 to 30 indicates a moderate exhibitionistic style with some frequent or severe reflective behaviors and attitudes; 11 to 20 indicates that your partner seldom has these behaviors and attitudes; and 0 to 10 indicates few or none of these.

Showing Off

Your partner may like to show off, be in the limelight, and have all eyes on him. His need to have attention and admiration includes you; in fact, he was probably drawn to you because you were able to give him the attention and admiration he craved. So, any hint that another person is getting your attention or admiration is very threatening to him, and his jealousy is aroused because of his fears of abandonment and destruction. An illustration of his behavior can be seen in your partner's irrational jealousy when you admire something about a public figure, such as a movie or television actor whom you will most likely never meet.

His desire and need to have all the attention and admiration involves you in another way. He expects you to stay in the background, never do or say anything that takes the attention away from him, and dress in a way that will not bring you attention. This allows him to remain front and center, showing his superiority and your inferiority. He can become hurt and enraged when you receive attention or admiration for even the smallest thing. For example, if someone were to remark that the cookies you had baked and sent to your child's class were very good, your partner might interject a statement to deflect the attention and compliment to him, such as commenting that he is glad you did not burn this batch like you often do, that the recipe is his mother's, or that he gave you the idea to bake the cookies. Nothing is off-limits for him if he can use it to show off.

The Biggest and the Best

Flamboyant, grand, and *extravagant* are terms that seem to fit the exhibitionistic style. People with this style have to have whatever is bigger and better than anyone else has, no matter what it is. It is only when they stand out in a way that shows their superiority that they can be pleased. They need other people's envy, deference, attention, and admiration, and they can become enraged when they don't receive this attention or it is given to someone else.

Requiring the biggest and the best can lead to overspending and financial difficulties. Below are some things exhibitionistic people may seek that require money and effort:

- physical perfection from plastic surgery
- a toned and fit body from physical exercise
- participation in community or political activities at the expense of family responsibilities
- extravagant parties and other events
- attendance at expensive or prestigious schools

Exhibitionistic people do not necessarily want these things; they get them because of their need for superiority and the opportunity to boast and brag.

If your partner fits this description, he expects you to unfailingly give him attention, be admiring of him and his accomplishments, display awareness of whatever he has that shows his superiority, envy him, and show him deference. You cannot lay it on too thick with this person, since he is confident that he deserves this, and even more.

Any hint that your attention, admiration, envy, and deference are shifting, lessening, or being given to someone else can lead him to become enraged. The jealousy emerges because the grandiose self is not strong enough to keep the impoverished self from seeping through and showing itself. The demand for attention is a part of his defense system to ward off any awareness of his impoverished self, which is deficient and shaming. The rage is a response to his feelings of deficiency and shame that, up to this point, he was able to repress and deny. The rage ensures that others are unable to see these unacceptable parts of him.

Boasting and Bragging

Your exhibitionistic partner is not reticent or shy about letting others know how wonderful he is. He boasts and brags at every opportunity. His is not a simple and understandable pride; it is an extreme and overwhelming pride that seems to consume him. Most everyone can feel pride when they achieve something of importance to them. This is universal, and it gives our confidence and self-esteem a boost. However, the person with an exhibitionistic style uses every opportunity to delineate his accomplishments, explain just how unique and special he is, and describe how these qualities put him above everyone else. He is adept at playing the one-upmanship game with the theme "anything you can do, I can do better.

He makes sure everyone knows that he is grand, extra-ordinary, and otherwise superior when he boasts and brags. For example, when he brags about his accomplishments, he makes sure that he explicitly or implicitly lets you know that it was creative, groundbreaking, heads and shoulders above what anyone else ever did, and worthy of a major prize. It does not matter how small, routine, ordinary, or expected the accomplishment was, it becomes magnificent and grand when he tells about it.

Perceiving himself in this way is one of the reasons he can become so hurt and enraged when he gets in touch with his jealousy. He is focused on his grandiose self, which he sees as expansive and superior, but the jealousy gets him in touch with his impoverished self, which encompasses his inadequacies, deficiencies, and shame. He feels that his obvious superiority in his eyes should be sufficient for you to not want or need anyone else in your life. This extends to family, friends, children, coworkers, and others. He is the center of his universe. Anything that challenges this grandiose self-perception is extremely threatening and can produce an overreaction. He, of course, does not see it that way and will resist all attempts to help him realize the irrationality of this response.

Unearned Credit

Your partner may have a tendency to try to take credit for things he didn't do, especially when attention and admiration are involved. He thinks that others were only able to accomplish something because of him and his contributions, no matter how far-fetched his view of his contribution may be. For example, if you were to achieve a promotion at work, it was because he had told you how to get it, not because of your hard work and accomplishments. This perception can also extend to your children—they never accomplish anything on their own; he always has a major role in whatever they achieve or do.

The tendency to claim unearned credit is also a part of his inflated, grandiose sense of who he is. He really believes that he is so powerful and knowing that you, and others, could not possibly achieve anything without him. Thus, he expects you to recognize how lucky you are to have him as a partner, and to never look at anyone else, even in a polite, social, or friendly way. Whenever your attention and adoration are not focused on him, he becomes anxious and enraged, fearing that he is not as superior and wonderful as he thinks he is. Since, in his mind, that cannot be true, the fault must be yours.

If you have ever tried to get your partner to recognize that he is trying to take unearned credit, or even just asked a question about his contribution, he probably just became hurt or angry. In his view, you should recognize and understand his contribution without his having to explain it. The fact that he cannot explain and did not actually contribute do not matter to him. In his mind, he did contribute, and no amount of rationality can convince him otherwise. He sees your questioning or challenging him as an affront, and he really does not appreciate that.

Since there will always be someone there who believes him, you are not going to be able to modify his behavior, and you are wasting your time and effort when you try to set the record straight. That does not help the relationship either. It's not easy to accept that there is little or nothing you can do to change his perceptions, attitudes, and behavior.

Subjugating Your Needs

The partner with an exhibitionistic style expects everyone in the world to do the following:

- play second fiddle

- understand that he always comes first

- give him preferential treatment

- recognize his superiority, uniqueness, and specialness

- sacrifice their needs for his

Most of all, he expects everyone, including you, to know and understand these needs and always act accordingly. This means that you too are expected to allow him to always be in first place for everything. To him, your needs, wants, and desires are of lesser importance, and you should know this and accept it.

Please remember that your partner is unaware of this expectation and attitude. He does not realize that he expects you to subjugate your needs; he just knows that when you don't, he becomes very anxious, upset, and even angry. So, trying to tell him about your perceptions, needs, and feelings can be futile.

In line with some of the other behaviors and attitudes on the scale, your partner will expect that the family resources will be used first for what he wants or needs, such as clothes, grooming, special equipment or tools, cars, and so on. Any necessary sacrifices so that he can have these resources should be made without question as far as he is concerned. If you were to feel or act any differently, he would not understand and would become hurt and angry. He feels that you are supposed to accept your role as second banana, and that others, such as children, are also supposed to defer to his wants, needs, and desires.

You may be comfortable with this role, and so subjugating your needs may not be a problem for you. In this case, you don't have to work at understanding; you just automatically give your partner preference. But if subjugation is not comfortable for you, you will need to find a way to have your needs receive priority some of the time.

Reacting to Being Ignored or Overlooked

Consistent with his need for attention, the exhibitionistic partner can become very upset whenever he feels he is ignored or overlooked. The upset can be expressed in a variety of ways such as the actions below:

- sulking and pouting

- starting a fight

- dropping or breaking something

- proposing that the group do something inappropriate, not planned, or offbeat

- telling an outrageous story or joke

- saying something offensive very loudly

Whatever the person does, it's calculated to bring him the attention he craves. He probably experiences intense jealousy and rage whenever he feels that you are ignoring or overlooking him, even when your attention is given to someone more needy, such as a child or a sick person. For that brief period he is not the center of your life, and he really feels that loss. These attitudes and feelings are not reasonable, rational, or logical, but they drive him in ways he does not understand. His fear of abandonment is closely tied to his sense of himself in the world; he may have a deep conviction that he will cease to exist if he is abandoned, and any lessening of attention triggers this conviction and fear. That is why some of the acting-out behaviors seem extreme, and why all of them are designed to get the life-supporting attention he feels is essential to survival.

In addition to acting out, your partner may become hurt, angry, and resentful that he had to remind you to give him the attention. This adds another layer of feelings that can be difficult to understand and to work through. Probably neither of you understands his actions and feelings, and you may focus only on their irrationality and unreasonableness. That focus is not helpful, since even if you are correct in terming his behavior unreasonable and irrational, he is not about to argue with you—it seems perfectly reasonable and logical to him. Think of this situation as one where you are using adult tactics and reasoning to try to deal with a two-year-old who wants his way. You do not win in that situation, and you will not win in this one.

Attention-Getting Behavior

Some of this was covered in the preceding discussion. The need for attention can be a primary motivator for much of what the person with an exhibitionistic style does and says. It's almost as if he is always shouting, "Look at me!"

You may have been attracted to your partner because he was flamboyant, charming, charismatic, larger than life, doing exciting things, exuberant, and able to get the attention you were not. He had characteristics you wanted, admired, or felt could be yours by association. Whatever your motivation was, you were drawn to him, and now he is your partner. Some of the characteristics that attracted you to him are now causing trouble in the relationship.

If your partner has an exhibitionistic style, when he becomes jealous, he will most likely act in whatever way he can to get attention. He will do such things as

- make a scene over something minor

- call attention to your behavior that signals to him your impending abandonment

- blatantly and outrageously retaliate by taking up with someone else

- start a fight with you or with the person he sees as a rival

- become verbally abusive to you or to the perceived rival

- openly sulk or pout so that there is no mistaking what he is doing

He may even walk out on you, but not before you and everyone else understand that he is displeased. He may call family members and friends to get their attention and sympathy over his plight, and to let everyone know just how you abandoned and hurt him. Whatever he is doing, he is always trying to get attention.

Seeking Compliments and Flattery

Your partner may go out of his way to get compliments and flattery. This behavior stems from his deep needs for attention and admiration, his desire to be thought of as unique and special, and even something of an entitlement attitude. Do not forget that these are deeply ingrained and enduring parts of his self, are primarily on the nonconscious and unconscious levels, and are used as reassurance that he exists and is worthy.

The people he encounters in his world play into his needs and he probably gets considerable compliments and flattery. If he does not, it is usually quite obvious because he becomes grumpy and dissatisfied with everything. Your partner also expects you to be unfailingly and consistently complimentary and flattering and, when you lapse, he is quick to let you know that you have dropped the ball.

Now, just about everyone can appreciate compliments, and many people like to be flattered. Your partner, however, is more extreme in his pursuit of these and will go to great lengths to get them. It's almost as if he thinks that he would disappear if others did not notice and comment on his superiority, uniqueness, and special qualities. Just being good enough, ordinary, and adequate does not seem to be sufficient; he has to stand out from everyone else almost all of the time.

Needing Recognition of Superiority

Does your partner do any of the following on a frequent basis?

- gives orders and expects them to be promptly obeyed
- requests favors, expects them to be fulfilled, but does not reciprocate
- thinks that others exist to serve him, meet his needs, and fulfill his desires
- expects his opinion, input, and the like to be accepted without question
- thinks that any question or disagreement is a personal attack or affront
- expects that other people should defer to him
- tends to exploit others
- seeks acknowledgment and affirmation of his power and control

- ensures that others know his acquisitions, achievements, and accomplishments

If you answered yes to three or more of these, then your partner is most likely actively searching for recognition of his superiority. He wants and needs the reassurance that recognition brings and, when it is not forthcoming, he can become very upset.

The person with the exhibitionistic style thinks of himself as superior and wants others to also perceive him as superior in every way. Most people can be satisfied with having some noteworthy moments or acts, but they do not expect to be seen as superior in every aspect of their life. The person with an exhibitionistic style does extend this expectation to everything. Thus, when he becomes jealous he is confronted with the twin possibilities that he is not as superior as he thinks he is, and that someone else is more superior. That is a very threatening possibility, which he fears will result in the destruction of his self. He will take almost any step to make sure that his self is safe and will not be destroyed. It can be helpful for you to recognize and accept just how essential and life-supporting is your partner's need to be recognized as superior. He cannot tolerate anything that suggests that he is not as superior and wonderful as he thinks he is.

Lack of Empathy

Your partner may seem to lack understanding of how other people feel. You may have characterized his attitude as indifferent, minimizing, devaluing, and the like when he has responded and reacted to your feelings and those of others. Have you ever tried to tell your partner about something that was important to you, only to have him

- dismiss it, saying that you are being oversensitive or overreacting
- ignore it completely and change the subject
- ask you to repeat it because he was not listening
- try to joke about it
- suggest that you were wrong for having these feelings
- tell you that you should be grateful for what you have
- compare you unfavorably with someone else

- call you unflattering names, such as whiner, crybaby, or wuss

All these responses demonstrate a lack of understanding or empathy for what you are feeling. But this may not be the most troubling part. If your partner has an exhibitionistic style, he is likely to both not understand your feelings and turn the conversation around so that it is now about him and his feelings.

Because your partner lacks empathy, he feels entitled to do and say whatever he pleases to other people. There may be times when he seems to try to understand what others are feeling and uses the proper words, but the feeling does not accompany the words. His feeling words are empty and void of real emotions. His only real interest is himself; others just don't appear on his radar screen except as they exist to serve him.

You will never be able to change this. Yes, people can develop empathy and some sensitivity to others' feelings, but that cannot be demanded or imposed externally. That development has to come from your partner's internal sources, and you don't have access to those. No amount of confronting, pleading, demanding, or modeling will cause or persuade your partner to understand what others are feeling.

You now have some information that enables you to possibly identify your partner's style of jealousy. Also discussed were some reactions and feelings you may experience in response to his expression of jealousy. Although he may be irrational and reacting to his unresolved issues and unfinished business, you are still left with your feelings and reactions, searching for possible solutions. Suggestions for furthering your self-development, understanding your partner, and defusing his jealousy are presented in the next chapter.

Chapter 8

Suggested Coping Strategies

This chapter presents some specific actions you can take to deal with your partner's jealousy. Some are general and can be used regardless of what category your partner seems to fit and others are targeted to a specific category. These are presented as guides. You did not cause the jealousy and you can't prevent it, but you can recognize and accept the underlying causes and resist becoming angry, hurt, or fearful. Much of what is presented below is intended to help you deal with your feelings when your partner becomes jealous. The following are some basic assumptions about you that provide a framework for suggested strategies:

- You do not deliberately do or say things to try to get a jealous reaction from your partner.

- Your partner's jealous reactions are troubling to you and to the relationship.

- Nothing you have done or said to this point has been effective in reducing or eliminating the jealousy.

- You are concerned about the lack of trust your partner's jealousy implies about you.

Other basic assumptions include the following:

- You cannot change your partner.

- The roots and causes of her jealousy lie in her fears of abandonment and destruction that are related to her family of origin experiences, past relationships, and personality.

- Your partner's self factors make significant contributions to her jealousy.

- The causes of jealousy are deep-seated and enduring.

Fifteen Suggested Strategies

The intended outcomes of the strategies listed below are to strengthen the relationship and to help you cope with your feelings aroused by your partner's jealousy. Many of the suggestions presented are "do nots," and it would be helpful if you would stop these behaviors, since they are not helping or being effective. You may already be doing some of the other suggested actions but are not getting the results you want. Don't stop doing these; adding some others may create a combination that will work. Read the following list and estimate how often you already use each strategy, and how you could use it in the future. Each item will be explained in this chapter.

1. Examine or reflect on my motives and behavior.

2. Ignore my partner's behavior.

3. Stay detached; keep my distance.

4. Use self-affirmations.

5. Remind myself of the irrationality of my partner's behavior.

6. Enhance my resources.

7. Make reasonable changes.

8. Don't retaliate.

9. Emotionally insulate myself from my partner's jealousy.

10. Take a time-out.

11. Give up the fantasy that my partner will change.

12. Accept that I cannot "fix" my partner.

13. Don't make a bad matter worse.

14. Leave relatives out of it.

15. Do not accept emotional or physical abuse.

Examine Your Motives and Behavior

Let's assume that you do not deliberately try to arouse your partner's jealousy. If for some reason you do this at times, please stop. That behavior is not at all helpful for the relationship. But, even if you do not do or say anything consciously, there may be an unconscious component. This is why we start with self-examination and self-reflection. You will want to explore for yourself if any of the needs listed below could be fueling your behavior, thoughts, or feelings in the relationship. These may be causing you to act in unconscious ways to try to arouse jealousy.

Exercise 17: My Motives

Procedure: Find a quiet place where you are unlikely to be disturbed. Get comfortable and close your eyes. Explore for yourself the extent of each of the following personal needs and their possible impact on your behavior:

- power and control needs

- attention needs

- admiration needs

- reassurance needs

- acceptance needs

Ask yourself the following questions about each:

1. How anxious or upset do I get when this need is in danger of not being met?

2. What do I do to get this need met?

3. How may I be using the relationship to get this need met?

You may find it helpful to write down your answers. Do not share your thoughts and answers with your partner, since these may give her additional ammunition. These are the thoughts, ideas, and feelings you can relate to a therapist or use for your own personal development.

This is your opportunity to be honest with yourself and to make changes if needed. You will want to work on any need you identify to contain and manage it better so that the relationship is not negatively affected, and to find more helpful and constructive ways to get it met.

Ignore Your Partner's Behavior

You may find it possible and helpful to ignore your partner's jealous behavior. To ignore does not mean that you are not affected or unaware of what is happening. You are very aware, but you understand the motive or intent of the jealous behavior even if your partner does not understand her jealousy. Since jealousy is irrational, you do not become irrational yourself in your response. Instead of responding to the irrationality, you ignore that part and respond to the underlying motive, such as a need for reassurance that she will not be abandoned. You can also ignore pouting and sulking behaviors and refuse to engage in fighting.

Stay Detached

A little distance and emotional detachment can keep you more balanced and prevent you from getting overwhelmed by or caught up in your partner's irrationality. This is not as easy to do as it may seem, because you are open to catching your partner's feelings. The closer or more connected you two are, the more open you will be to catching her anger, hurt, and other feelings. Once you catch these, your own feelings can get triggered, and you may even identify with the caught feelings and act on them. For example, you were not angry before the interaction, but now you are angry. Staying detached can help reduce some of the intensity of what is caught, identified with, and acted on.

How do you stay detached? By using a couple of effective strategies: emotional insulation and thinking. Emotional insulation is explained later in the chapter. Thinking, when done to prevent yourself from joining in the irrational jealous behavior, simply means that you make a conscious effort to think about what is happening, what your partner's behavior signals about her fears, and how best to respond. Whenever you sense that your feelings are intensifying and escalating, you can tell yourself to stop and think.

Use Self-Affirmations

These can be very helpful in a variety of circumstances. Self-affirmations are reminders of your efficacy, worth, value, esteem, and confidence. You may forget your more positive attributes when faced with the demeaning, devaluing, and hurtful comments your partner makes when she is jealous. Self-affirmations can also help you deal with your own anxiety and fear around abandonment and destruction. Here are some examples of self-affirmations:

I can take care of myself.

I don't have to have everyone like me and approve of me in order to be adequate.

I can manage and control my anxiety.

I have a lot of strengths.

Remind Yourself of the Behavior's Irrationality

It can be helpful to stop and think to remind yourself of the irrationality of your partner's jealousy. Remind yourself not to buy into her irrationality, not to allow your faulty assumptions to contribute, and not to act on irrational thoughts you may have about yourself. When you do any of these, you can start to assume responsibility for your partner's jealousy when the responsibility really is hers. If you can stop your slide into irrational thoughts and avoid getting caught up in the intense emotions, you can make wiser and more effective responses.

Enhance Your Resources

This is a complex topic that cannot be adequately presented here. Your own personal resources are internal. When you develop these, you will be more centered, grounded, confident, and effective. Everyone can use some personal development to enhance their resources, and this is a lifelong process. These resources include

- developing any aspects of underdeveloped narcissism that may linger

- building strong and resilient psychological boundaries

- integrating and accepting the "good" and "bad" parts of oneself

- freely choosing values and beliefs

- being creative

- seeking inspiration or spirituality

There are many avenues to developing your self and you will want to find the ones that best suit your needs.

Make Reasonable Changes

You could make some reasonable changes in your behavior if you find that you are unconsciously doing things that you would rather not do, and that these behaviors are contributing to your partner's distress. For example, you can become aware of how much time you actually spend with a particular person or the number of times you quote someone; you can pay attention to ways in which you may be taking your partner for granted and not showing appreciation; you can compliment her more often or do some of the things you did when you first met.

You do not have to make drastic or major changes, just some thoughtful ones. Focus on positive changes, such as being more thoughtful and sensitive. You should not force yourself to make changes that do not feel right, such as cutting a family member out of your life. If that family member is undermining your confidence or your relationship, then cutting them out could be helpful, but only if you are doing it for yourself and not in response to the demands of your partner.

Don't Retaliate

Few things are more destructive to a relationship than retaliation. Getting back at your partner is not a mature, helpful, or responsible reaction to her jealousy. Even if she is out of line in the way she chooses to express her jealousy, such as trying to start a fight, you can be more mature and constructive if you refrain from retaliation.

Think of it this way: Retaliation may feel empowering to you, but a meaningful and satisfying relationship cannot survive these revengeful behaviors. They erode the quality of the relationship, promote distrust, and can fuel an escalation of hostility. You may win in the short term and derive some satisfaction from your partner's discomfort, but there is a negative long-term effect. If you are tempted to retaliate, work on your power and control issues instead.

Insulate Yourself Emotionally

This can be one of your most helpful strategies. Emotional insulation can help protect you from catching your partner's emotions and projections. It can keep you from identifying with her projections or getting mired in your negative emotions aroused when your partner becomes jealous. You can remain calmer, more grounded, and more centered during these times, and that can help you make more constructive and positive responses. The following exercise can help you begin the process of developing emotional insulation.

Exercise 18: Protection

Materials: A sheet of drawing paper and a set of crayons, felt markers, or colored pencils.

Procedure: Find a quiet place to work where you can draw without interruption or distraction.

1. Sit in silence and visualize something that will protect you while still allowing you to see and hear the other person. This something can be a wall, gate, shade, force field, curtain, shield, or whatever you choose.

2. As you visualize your protective object, explore it in detail, noting its shape, color, height, depth, and other characteristics.

3. When you have your protective object fixed in your mind, open your eyes and draw it. This helps to make it more substantial and real.

4. The final step is to use your emotional insulation judiciously so as to maintain your equanimity but not lose the more positive aspects of the relationship and intimacy. If your partner is prone to attacking or displaying intense negative feelings, you may find that the emotional

insulation prevents you from joining in, getting upset, or saying things you wish you had not said.

Take a Time-Out

When you find yourself being drawn into the emotional vortex, you can use a time-out to collect yourself, to begin thinking instead of feeling, and to get your emotional insulation in place. You don't have to take a long time; even a few seconds may suffice. It's probably most helpful if you can leave the presence of your partner, but if that is not possible, you can take a psychological and emotional time-out. Some possible ways of taking a quick time-out include

- going to the bathroom

- coughing or blowing your nose

- dropping something

- getting distracted

- looking away from your partner

- moving to sit down or stand up

- suggesting that you move to another location to continue the conversation

- straightening your clothes, hair, and so on.

Use the time-out to think, employ your emotional insulation, or make some self-affirmations.

Give Up the Fantasy That Your Partner Will Change

You may wish that your partner would change, or you may believe that you can say or do something to prompt her to change. These are fantasies, and by engaging in them you are wasting time and effort that could be put to more constructive use. Your relationship, and you personally, will be helped more when you give up your fantasy that your partner will change.

This does not mean that your partner cannot change; she can. She will change when she sees the need to change and when her inner self wants to change. It cannot be imposed from the outside; she is in charge of making changes. But she will also have difficulty making changes until she understands the effects of her past experiences and underdeveloped narcissism on her attitudes and behaviors. You don't have the expertise to guide her in the discovery process, nor can you force, demand, or push her to do this. It is not in your power or under your control.

Accept That You Cannot "Fix" Your Partner

Some people have a strong need or desire to "fix" other people. They may want to repair what is hurt or broken, soothe, give advice, show others the error of their ways, tell them what they should or ought to do, or provide a prescription for what they say needs fixing.

"Fixing" is intended to help the other person, but its underlying intent is to make the other person over in the image of what the fixer wants. In effect, you are not recognizing her as a separate and unique individual; you are assuming that she needs to be the kind of person you want her to be. This too is a fantasy. You must accept that you cannot "fix" another person. Any changes she makes will have to come from within.

Don't Make a Bad Matter Worse

When your partner displays jealousy, it can be very easy to make a bad matter worse with your responses. Poor responses are not thought through; they are spontaneous and are done without regard for their impact or consequences. The responses also affect you, and that is an often-overlooked consequence. The undesirable consequences fall into three categories: fight, flight, and making it personal. *Fight responses* are those that go on the offensive, usually to retaliate, exact revenge, or prevent further attacks. Examples of fight responses are

- negative comments about her personal characteristics, failings, errors, and the like

- devaluing and demeaning comments

- sarcasm

- behaviors designated to humiliate or embarrass

Flight responses are those that involve psychologically and emotionally leaving. There are times when it may be best for all concerned if you physically remove yourself from the situation, but there are also times when physical leaving is contraindicated. Examples of flight behaviors and attitudes that are not helpful include the following:

- bringing another person into the conflict

- sulking and pouting

- flouncing off in a huff

- refusing to give what she said or did any consideration

- ignoring her, not just the behavior

- becoming cold and distant

Making it personal means that you take the comments of your jealous partner as valid attacks on your value, worth, and lovability. You assume that she is right, and that you are flawed and wrong. This response is not helpful to your self-confidence and self-esteem. This response also indicates that you are not giving her the responsibility for her feelings, and that you feel responsible for how she feels. This is an assumption and attitude you could work on for yourself.

Leave Relatives Out

Some families are so close that they get involved in each other's struggles. It can be helpful and comforting to know that you have these resources available to you for encouragement and support. That is the healthy version of a close family. The not-so-healthy version is enmeshment—when what happens to one family member happens to all family members, and they do not perceive each other's differences. It is more helpful to your relationship with your partner if you leave your relatives out of the conflict.

With a healthy close family, the members will listen to you, encourage and support you, and affirm your relationship with your partner, but they would not go any further if you were to ask them to get involved. With an enmeshed or not-so-healthy family, members will take your side, dismiss and denigrate your partner, and let her know that they don't think much of her. This may be comforting to you, but it does not help the relationship, and it can be even more upsetting to your partner. Unless the situation is life threatening or extremely serious, it is best to leave relatives out of it.

Do Not Accept Emotional and Physical Abuse

When your partner becomes jealous, do you think, feel, or believe any of the following?

- It is your fault if she is angry or unhappy.

- You need interdependence, because independence is scary.

- You were not as attentive as you should have been.

- It is critical that you have an intimate connection, and you will do anything to keep it.

- You examine your behavior for causes of your partner's behaviors.

- You make excuses for what your partner does or says when she is angry or upset.

- You consider that it is your responsibility alone to preserve the relationship.

- You try to cope with your partner's feelings before taking care of your own.

If you answered yes to any of these items, you will want to explore for yourself whether you are setting yourself up to take or excuse emotional or physical abuse. If you are overly fearful of not having a partner, feel that almost everything that gets your partner upset can be traced to your failure or your being not good enough, or feel that you need to change so that your partner will be happy, you may find yourself in a situation where you are doing or accepting self-destructive behavior and attitudes. The situation is not good for you or for children who may be present. You are responsible for your well-being, and your partner is responsible for hers. You do not have to accept emotional or physical abuse.

Handling the Jealous Tirade

Your partner may demonstrate her distress with a tirade or by withdrawing and giving you the silent treatment. Following are some suggestions for handling the immediate situation. These are divided into two categories: things not to do and things to do.

Things Not to Do

- verbally analyze her motives, behaviors, etc.

- change the topic

- get caught up in her irrationalities

- become angry and upset

- let your nurturing self take over

Don't Analyze

One of the most inflammatory things you can do when your partner is expressing or demonstrating her jealousy nonverbally is to analyze out loud what she is doing. You may be tempted to tell her why you think she is jealous, assuming of course that you do understand, in an effort to get her to see how irrational she is. To do this is the equivalent of throwing gasoline on a bonfire. Instead, you can silently analyze her actions; this will help keep you from getting caught up in the irrationality or emotional intensity.

Don't Change the Topic

Don't think you can defuse your partner's jealousy and its accompanying emotions by changing the topic. You may think that she will be more rational and less emotionally intense later and try to delay having to respond to her jealousy. But what is more likely to happen is that your partner will feel devalued, that her concerns are minimized or even ignored, that you don't care, or that her feelings are not important to you. None of these are helpful to the relationship, and the already intense negative feelings can become even more intense.

If you do think that a change of topic would be helpful in the short term, it is best to at least acknowledge her concerns and feelings first, announce that you want to delay a discussion until a specified time, and communicate that you are committed to working this out with her. Try to get her approval or agreement to change the topic. This strategy can acknowledge some of her underlying concerns about the relationship without making her feel as if you are brushing her off.

Don't Get Caught Up in the Irrationality

You may have some emotional susceptibility to your partner and become caught up in the irrationality of her jealousy. You will find that both of you will then become increasingly more irrational, without knowing how to stop the fast slide into greater irrationality. It is hard to shut off once it gets started, and your partner is less able to stop than you are, since she is likely to be more emotionally intense.

Your emotional insulation is most helpful to keep you from catching the irrationality, but it can happen so fast that you are unprepared to block it by using your shield, force field, or other protective device (see exercise 18, earlier in this chapter). You are not prepared for your partner's jealousy, or for her feelings that accompany it. Employing your emotional insulation after you catch her emotions is not as effective as being prepared, but it can still be helpful. Once you realize what is happening, you can employ your emotional insulation. That will help from this point on.

The other strategy that can help is to try to think even though you have caught some feelings that are uncomfortable and intense. Think about what you are feeling, what aroused those feelings, the possibility that you caught the feelings, and what is the most helpful response you can make under the circumstances.

Don't Become Angry and Upset

You can contain and manage your emotions if you choose. You do not have to become angry and upset. If your partner is angry and upset, your becoming so only adds to your mutual distress. There are many good reasons to work to reduce or eliminate these feelings even when you are right and your partner is being unreasonable and wrong.

This does not mean that you should repress or deny your feelings. It could be helpful in the short term to contain and manage them: to suppress them, to not express them, and to act as if you did not experience them. You may have these feelings, but you don't let them control you, cause you to say imprudent things you may later regret, or make you lash out at your partner. You can work on a long-term objective to not feel threatened so that you do not become angry and upset as part of your personal development.

Don't Nurture

This particular "don't" is meant for people who take responsibility for other people's feelings, thinking that they must do something to make the other person feel better. Yes, you care about your partner, you want her to stop having these uncomfortable feelings and to have more pleasant ones, but you are not helping yourself when you allow your nurturing self to emerge when your partner is jealous. You are simply reinforcing her behavior. However, you are not providing the reassurance she craves even though that may be your intent. What is actually taking place is called *soothing*, much like what a parent gives to a child. Since you are in an adult relationship, you need treat your partner as an adult; hence, soothing is not beneficial in the long run.

Things to Do: Internal Actions

There are some tactics and strategies that can be helpful in the immediate situation, and we now turn to them. These are divided into two categories: internal feelings and thoughts, and external actions and responses. You can use the following inner resources to help you cope and defuse your partner's jealousy. They are reminders of what your partner's underlying reasons are for her jealousy and provide support for your self and help keep you centered and grounded.

- Do remember that you are not your partner's parent.
- Remind yourself that retaliation is not an option.
- Leave others out of the conflict.
- Accept that your partner may switch from the grandiose self to the impoverished without notice.
- Stay in touch with your thoughts and feelings.

Remember That You Are Not a Parent

Why is this necessary? You know that you are not your partner's parent, and she also knows that. It may seem unnecessary and silly to say something like this, but you may be using nonconscious and unconscious behaviors and attitudes that reflect the parental role and not the equal adult role. Yes, your partner may act childish at times, but that is not a signal for you to assume the parental role.

The adult role is one in which you expect and allow her to take responsibility for her actions, thoughts, feelings, and ideas.

Avoid Retaliation

You may find it necessary at some point to remind yourself that it is not helpful to retaliate. You may want to hurt her just like she is hurting you, but that is not helpful for you or for the relationship.

If you should contemplate retaliation, you can stop at that point and consider the pros and cons for doing this. You can win, but you could lose, and both of you could end up being angry, hurt and upset. You don't have to respond by acting childish yourself, or by assuming the parental role.

Leave Others Out

Don't let the thought even cross your mind to bring others into the conflict or the jealous tirade. Few would want to be a part of this kind of conflict, and the few who would want to be involved would not do or say anything helpful for the relationship. Your motive may be to try to involve someone whom your partner might listen to and be influenced by. She might give in and agree with this person at this point, but she would carry some lingering resentment toward both of you for getting support for your "side."

Accept Your Partner's Switches

Your partner may easily and swiftly switch from one state to the other without warning, and this can be very disconcerting. For example, she may start off in the grandiose state by saying something like "How dare you do this to me," only to switch to the impoverished state with her next comment by saying something like, "I guess I'm not good enough for you." You can stay very busy, and very ineffective, responding to these, and the switching adds to your internal confusion and anxiety. You can quickly get to the point where you don't know how to respond, since her next comment always seems to catch you off guard.

Don't try to anticipate or respond to either state. If you can stay centered and grounded and make your responses calm, mild, and in the general area of her comments, you can defuse much of her anxiety. For example, to the first comment that came from the grandiose state, you could respond with something like this: "You're offended by something you think I did," or "I can see that you're upset." A response to the second comment from the impoverished state could be, "I gave you my heart because you were good enough," or "You're my darling no matter what comes along." The task is to just accept that she will switch, and to not try to keep up with the switches.

Stay in Touch with Your Thoughts and Feelings

Practice staying in touch with your thoughts and feelings during interactions with your partner when she is jealous. Yes, you do want to reach out to her, but you will be more effective if you can tune in to what you are thinking and feeling at the same time. When you can tap in to your current thoughts and feelings you can

- remind yourself to not respond in kind
- use your emotional shielding
- make self-affirming statements
- get a handle on what your partner may be experiencing
- analyze immediate interactions
- think of constructive responses
- not get caught up in her irrationality
- realize when you may be catching her feelings

Things to Do: External Actions

Below is the final set of constructive behaviors and attitudes, external actions that may help defuse the jealous tirade:

- Use a soft, calm voice tone.
- Reaffirm the relationship.
- Maintain eye contact.
- Try to relax.
- Don't become defensive or overexplain.

Soften Your Voice Tone

The best strategy to reduce emotional intensity is a soft and calm voice tone. When you use this voice tone you convey confidence, steadfastness, and assurance. You can also convey caring and concern, especially when combined with other nonverbal gestures. These messages can do much to reassure your partner when she is in the grip of strong emotions and irrational thoughts.

Using a calm, soft voice tone may take some effort on your part, since you may be very tense and anxious when she challenges you with her jealous comments. However, if you can put your feelings on hold for the moment, use your emotional shielding, and think of how best to respond and handle the situation, you may be able to force or allow your voice to be calm and soft. The strategies for relaxing later on in the chapter can assist you with this.

Reaffirm the Relationship

Since your partner is fearful of abandonment or destruction of her self, it could be helpful to reaffirm the relationship when she is feeling jealous. That does not mean that you should gush reassurances, since that might just be cause for more suspicion. What is more helpful is to convey your affection on an adult-to-adult basis. That can mean a special touch or signal between the two of you, the smile or wink that says "you're great," a quick and quiet whisper about how good she looks, looking at her and smiling while you're talking to someone else, or anything that could be a sign that she is special to you.

If she is in the midst of a jealous tirade, you can best reassure her by not overreacting or becoming defensive. A quiet, reassuring remark about your commitment to her and to the relationship will be sufficient for the moment.

Maintain Eye Contact

Your face communicates your feelings. This is true for most people, although some have schooled their faces to hide what they are really thinking or feeling. This is an example of the "false self" discussed in chapter 5. Your face can also reveal your real self, and your eyes are the most expressive part of your face. This is one reason why it can be important to maintain eye contact, so that your partner does not lose sight of your real feelings about her and the relationship.

It can be important for you not to use sustained eye contact to intimidate, force, demand, or communicate in other negative ways. You may be angry, exasperated, or upset, but you do want to take care that your eye contact is reaffirming of the relationship and not used to put your partner on the defensive or to get her to do what you want her to. This is another opportunity to use your thinking skills to try to defuse her jealousy.

Try to Relax

The more you can communicate being relaxed, the better you will be able to reduce your partner's emotional intensity. Body tension is a response to a perceived threat, whether that threat is real or imagined. Thus, when your partner exhibits or expresses jealousy and you do not respond by becoming tense in preparation to fight or flee, your partner receives the message that you are centered, grounded, and in control of yourself. It can also communicate that she is off target with her jealousy. Further, being relaxed can help you mobilize your inner resources, such as thinking and emotional insulation.

It may be hard to relax when your partner is sending you powerful and intense feelings and you are catching all or part of them. You can find that you tense up despite your efforts to remain relaxed. To stay relaxed, concentrate on your breathing and try to make it deep and even. Take a deep breath, become aware of how that feels, and slowly release it. This can calm and relax you. Keep your focus on your breathing and consciously try to make it deep and even.

Avoid Becoming Defensive

You may be tempted to explain your actions in an attempt to defuse the situation or show your partner that she has made an error. Explaining is not helpful at this point, since your partner is in the grip of irrationality. She will not hear, understand, or accept much of what you try to explain. Indeed, she may use your explanation as evidence that she is correct, thinking that if she were incorrect you would not have a need to defend yourself.

If you are the kind of person who launches into explanations in an effort to get others to understand something, you can help yourself and your partner if you modify this behavior. Don't voluntarily explain, because many people think this is a sign of defensiveness; that is, you've done something wrong, and you are now trying to defend your actions. A better strategy is to make a simple statement and stop. Wait for the other person to ask for more information instead of trying to tell her what you think she needs to know or wants to hear under the circumstances.

Strategies for Specific Styles

The foregoing are some general responses that you can select to fit the circumstance and your partner. You will develop others as you think about the situation and the various factors as they fit you and your partner. Here are specific strategies that you can use to deal with the different styles of jealousy.

Clingy Style

This person's fears of abandonment are easily accessed and are very intense. Therefore, the best strategies will focus on addressing that fear in a direct way.

- Give her your full attention while she is talking to you.

- Reassure her of your commitment to the relationship.

- Soothe her with comforting words.

- Don't offer physical affections; save that for later.

Although you are responding to childish behavior, you don't want to treat her as you would a child, such as hugging her. This can have the intended effect at that moment, but it can carry a message that you don't understand, are not taking her seriously, and are not addressing the basic fear. Wait until both of you are ready for an adult type of affection.

Reactive Style

If this style fits your partner, she is fearful of destruction of her self, skeptical, and cynical because of her many negative experiences in previous relationships. She will tend to mistrust your responses, so you have to be careful when selecting a response. It is very important that you not buy into her emotionality, which would increase her skepticism and mistrust. Here are some suggested strategies:

- Stay calm and somewhat detached.

- Don't take her negative comments about you personally.

- Don't use soothing strategies.

- Be consistent and genuine.

Your calmness and somewhat detached behavior can help settle her down, keep you from catching her emotions, and give you time to think of a verbal response. She can make negative comments about you that are hurtful as well as being untrue. Your detachment can help you to see that her lashing out is how she protects her impoverished self from greater disappointment. It is not helpful to try to soothe her, since this can make her even more suspicious. Whatever your response, be sure to be calm, measured, consistent, and genuine.

Manipulative Style

Never forget that your partner will try to manipulate you for reasons that you don't know or understand, and that may also be hidden from her. She uses some manipulation that is deliberate, and some that is unconscious. Understanding this can help you implement the following strategies:

- Ignore childish behaviors, such as pouting and sulking.

- Refuse to engage her when she goes on the offensive.

- Don't try to reassure or joke her out of jealousy.

- Don't let her exaggerations trigger your anger, hurt, or resentment.

What you are really doing when you implement these strategies is refusing to be manipulated. You are calling a halt to being manipulated, and you are not using manipulative behaviors yourself. You are acting as an adult, not as a child or as her parent. It is a very powerful strategy to use with someone who has a manipulative style: you do not use manipulation when responding to her manipulation, since that could intensify her fear of destruction.

Exhibitionistic Style

Your partner uses theatrical techniques to grab the spotlight. Her fears of abandonment and destruction of self are very acute and can emerge at any time. She needs external confirmation of her existence to bolster her internal fear that she is not real and may cease to exist at any second. The strategies below take this need of hers into account. If you can remember her deep-seated and enduring fears, you can implement the following strategies:

- Give her your full and undivided attention for the moment.

- Compliment her on something unrelated to the outburst of jealousy.

- Reaffirm the relationship.

- Try to reduce the emotional intensity with calm and quiet responses.

Your full and undivided attention is best conveyed with non-verbal gestures. Turn your body to face her, obtain eye contact, and make sure your facial expression is pleasant and relaxed and shows interest in her alone for this period of time. You don't want to change the topic, but find some way to compliment her that is unrelated to her outburst of jealousy. Don't say things like "I love it when your eyes flash like that—it's so thrilling," or "You're better than she [the target of her jealousy] is." These are the types of statements that can make her suspicious of your intent. Select something unrelated for your compliment, such as "I was thinking earlier that you do so many things to make our life run smoothly, but I don't tell you that I appreciate it." Reaffirm the relationship, and work to reduce her emotional intensity; this will also help to reduce your anxiety and tension.

A Final Word

We've arrived at the end of this book and it may be helpful to summarize the major objectives and intents to see if they were accomplished. The major premises of this book are that you do not cause your partner's jealousy and that you do not have the power to change her. If you can accept these two premises, then you are well on your way to addressing your partner's jealousy in a constructive way. As a result, you can prevent yourself from getting caught up in the intense emotions and irrationality of your partner's jealousy. You are able to think of viable responses that are helpful. Her behavior and attitudes are more understandable to you because you understand the possible effects of her family of origin experiences and other negative past experiences on her. You can set reasonable limits for yourself. Your psychological boundaries can become stronger and more resilient. You become empowered in the relationship and more committed to it.

References

Brown, N. W. 2001. *Children of the Self-Absorbed*. Oakland, Calif.: New Harbinger Publications.

———. 2002. *Whose Life Is It Anyway? When to Stop Taking Care of Their Feelings and Start Taking Care of Your Own*. Oakland, Calif.: New Harbinger Publications.

Masterson, J. G. 1993. *The Emerging Self: A Developmental, Self, and Object Relations Approach to the Treatment of the Closet Narcissistic Disorder of the Self*. New York: Brunner Mazel.

Winnicott, D. W. 1960. The theory of the parent-infant relationship. In *Maturational Processes and the Facilitating Environment*. New York: International Universities Press.

Some Other
New Harbinger Titles

The Power of Two Workbook, Item 3341 $19.95

Adult Children of Divorce, Item 3368 $14.95

Fifty Great Tips, Tricks, and Techniques to Connect with Your Teen, Item 3597 $10.95

Helping Your Child with OCD, Item 3325 $19.95

Helping Your Depressed Child, Item 3228 $14.95

The Couples's Guide to Love and Money, Item 3112 $18.95

50 Wonderful Ways to be a Single-Parent Family, Item 3082 $12.95

Caring for Your Grieving Child, Item 3066 $14.95

Helping Your Child Overcome an Eating Disorder, Item 3104 $16.95

Helping Your Angry Child, Item 3120 $17.95

The Stepparent's Survival Guide, Item 3058 $17.95

Drugs and Your Kid, Item 3015 $15.95

The Daughter-In-Law's Survival Guide, Item 2817 $12.95

Whose Life Is It Anyway?, Item 2892 $14.95

It Happened to Me, Item 2795 $17.95

Act it Out, Item 2906 $19.95

Parenting Your Older Adopted Child, Item 2841 $16.95

Boy Talk, Item 271X $14.95

Talking to Alzheimer's, Item 2701 $12.95

Helping a Child with Nonverbal Learning Disorder or Asperger's Syndrome, Item 2779 $14.95

The 50 Best Ways to Simplify Your Life, Item 2558 $11.95

When Anger Hurts Your Relationship, Item 2604 $13.95

Call **toll free, 1-800-748-6273,** or log on to our online bookstore at **www.newharbinger.com** to order. Have your Visa or Mastercard number ready. Or send a check for the titles you want to New Harbinger Publications, Inc., 5674 Shattuck Ave., Oakland, CA 94609. Include $4.50 for the first book and 75¢ for each additional book, to cover shipping and handling. (California residents please include appropriate sales tax.) Allow two to five weeks for delivery.

Prices subject to change without notice.